Travel to Cinque Terre, Italy Tour

Sights and Attractions

Lucas Ball.

Publisher:
SONIT
2162 Davenport House, 261 Bolton Road. Bury. Lancashire. BL8 2NZ. United Kingdom.

Table of Content

Summary

On the surface, travel is about seeing new places and (if you're heading abroad to volunteer) giving a bit back at the same time. But underneath it is so much more, opening your horizons to experience completely different cultures, cuisines and landscapes. While photos are proof that you went and saw, it's the transformation that takes place within that is often the strongest evidence of why travel is important.

Some argue that it's an indulgent expense, spending money to travel that could be spent saving for a home loan or "building for the future", but travel addicts would debate a strong case against this. It's not about ticking off the "bucket list" and being able to recount all the countries you've visited, but the way travel impacts you as a person, your interactions with others and your humanity towards the rest of the world.

So if you need a little help convincing yourself or others why traveling is a worthy pursuit, here are ten reasons why it's important.

Introduction

Cinque Terre, Porto Venere and the three Island of Palmaria, Tino and Tinetto are inserts on the UNESCO World Heritage List, chosen for being distinguished exemplars of the ways in which man has been able to model and transform the environment here, without, however, altering the beauty of the landscape.

Historic, spectacular, multi-colored borgoes overlooking the Mediterranean Sea, nestled between rocky reliefs and steep cliffs that are a sheer drop away from the coast, terraced hillsides where world-famous vineyards triumph this is the Cinque Terre, in Liguria: Monterosso, Vernazza, Corniglia, Manarola, and Riomaggiore.

Seaside villages surrounded by agricultural terrain, they are rich in color, charm and simplicity, and make up part of the protected area of the Cinque Terre National Park.

Monterosso is a famous touristic locality, fascinating for its elegant villas and gorgeous Fegina Beach. Narrow streets the so-called caruggi that clamber towards the old center where the Gothic-style Parochial

Church of San Giovanni Battista rises, along with the 17th-Century Church of St. Francis, annexed to a Capuchin Monastery. Monterosso is also the site of the "literary park" dedicated to the poet and bard of these lands, Eugenio Montale.

Vernazza is a beautiful borgo that developed around its little port, already well-known and frequented during the Roman Age.

Among its characteristic spots are the little piazza right on the sea and the Gothic, two-story church dedicated to Santa Margherita of Antioch. Dominating Vernazza from above is the Doria Castle, erected to defend against naval attacks. It boasts a lookout tower, considered the twin of a tower constructed on the walking trail leading to Corniglia.

Corniglia lies 100 meters (328 feet) above the sea on the rocky ridge of a promontory; it is connected to the beach by a 365-step stairway. The population in and around Corniglia traditionally occupy themselves with wine cultivation, as witnessed by the typical terraces that are characteristic of the terrain between Genoa and Tuscany. The grand abilities of Italians in cultivation and engineering since the Medieval Age also confirm themselves in this area.

Manarola soars over an enormous pile of black boulders, so that the colored houses seem to spring up right out of the rocks.

Other than for its beauty, Manarola is oft-noted for its excellent oil and sought-after passito wine, "Sciachetrà."

The last Cinque Terre is Riomaggiore, the heart of the same-named Park. Riomaggiore is a picturesque fishing village, with high, narrow houses typically in pastel tones, and a breathtakingly natural chiaroscuro that is aided in party by the tight and winding caruggi.

The other location making up part of the UNESCO World Heritage Site is Porto Venere. An elegant vacation and resort destination, it is a perfect union between nature and architecture, and features a delightful touristic port, similarly to the rest of its Ligurian neighbors. An infinite array of colors decorate its houses, precipitous staircases and tiny alleys. The pretty Church of San Pietro, peeking out over the Promontory near the Bocche sea, was built in the Paleo-Christian epoch, and eventually re-worked in the Gothic style.

From here visitors can take in a fantastic panoramic view.

Also rather particular are the Sanctuary of the White Madonna, previously the Romanesque Parochial Church of San Lorenzo erected in the 12th Century, and later restored and enlarged; and the Doria Castle, a majestic military fort.

Across the sea from Porto Venere sit the three Islands of Palmaria, Tino and Tinetto, all making up part of the Regional Park of Portovenere.

Palmaria is the largest and most-appreciated by tourists, especially to visit the Blue Grotto (or Grotta Azzurra) by boat. The magnificent villages of the Cinque Terre are abundant in historical and cultural prestige, and welcome visitors to their unique scenery with extraordinary vistas of the waterfront and of their singular natural endowments.

The history of Cinque Terre

The history of the Cinque Terre, five small fishing villages situated on steep cliffs, goes far back in time. The name "Cinque Terre" dates back to before the fifteenth century but the history of the coast on which the small villages are located dates far back. The primitive man lived in this stretch of land, approximately 18 km long, between sea and mountains and proof of this are the antique remains, such as bones and prehistorical instruments found.

The ancient Romans conquered this area by taking it with great difficulty from the stubborn population of Liguria. Harsh battles fought on a hostile war round that was a tempting conquest for who aspired to strategic positions on the Mediterranean Sea. In this way the small piece of land extending from Montenero to Mesco Point for centuries went through the anger of ruthless populations of different empires, all having in common the desire of making the Golfo della Luna (Gulf of the Moon) and the confining lands theirs. The also called Golfo di Venere (Gulf of Venus), already extol by the ancient poets for the natural beauty of its landscape, appeared as a natural gulf, protected by the rage of the sea and of the wind.

The Cinque Terre stretch from the western part of the Gulf of La Spezia, confining with Portovenere, historical stronghold of the Genoese Republic. Even earlier, this maritime centre had been besieged by the barbaric tribes coming from the north of Europe, then by Byzantines, by Lombards and in the twelfth century by Genoa that for centuries battled against Pisa to defend its own maritime bastion. The coast, where the five small villages rise today, was not extraneous to commercial and military interests so that from the beginning of the tenth century, the first signs of transformation of this territory, naturally wild and hostile to man, showed. The inhabitants of the hinterland of the coast, and in particular those coming from the Valley of Vara began to settle on the coast which once again was safe after the incursions of the Saracens of the past centuries.

The first villages next to the sea were constructed. A radical and hard transformation process took place and during this man broke rock from the mountains overlooking the sea, separated by narrow valleys without any floodplains. A dry and barren land where the people of Liguria wanted to invest to create new life conditions. From the broken rock, only the biggest pieces were chosen for the construction of dry-stone walls and the smaller ones were used to make the soil fertile by creating a humus cultivable by adding scrub and pine-needles. It was a challenge against a hostile nature, a conquest that has lasted for more than nine centuries and requiring continuous interventions. On the "dry-stone walls", symbol of the Cinque Terre, rows of vines, of olive and citrus trees are the only precious gift given to a dry land which nevertheless is generous in the quality of its products.

After the conquer of the land, comes the conquer of the sea, the immense blue spread that surrounds the coast and the inaccessible cliffs. The people of the Cinque Terre from farmers became sailors fought in 1170 with the Republic of Genoa in the battle against Pisa. These are the first sea battles to which the inhabitants of the Cinque Terre take part, ready to jealously defend what they have conquered thanks to their constant and hard work.

In the villages, the buildings are constructed as house-towers, high and narrow, like small fortresses to protect against unexpected dangers coming from the sea: an unknown sea that strikes fear but that excites the tenacity of those who are used to struggling. The adventure of searching for new stimulus, that the sea can offer, was seen as a new challenge.

The ships, that often appear at the horizon in the waters of the gulf, bring hope of new interests, in new activities for living. In this way the commercial activities tied to fishing, together with agriculture main activity of the economy of the Cinque Terre, flourish.

Riviera di Levante and the Cinque Terre

Liguria can be found in north-west Italy. It is a long, narrow coastal region running from the tuscan border all the way to France. Its setting is stunning, it lies between the Ligurian Sea and the mountains (Maritime Alps and the Apennines). The whole region is like a huge green terrace with breathtaking sea view.

The Ligurian Riviera - also called Italian Riviera - is divided into two main parts by its capital city, Genova: the Riviera di Ponente - the coast of the setting sun - to the west, and the Riviera di Levante - the coast of the rising sun - to the east. The Riviera di Ponente is elegant, full of nice holiday resorts, sandy beaches and bigger towns. The Riviera di Levante is my kind of place. It is wilder, more rugged and rustic, full of promontories, hidden bays and colourful seaside villages: the Cinque Terre, Tellaro, Portovenere, Portofino, Camogli...just a few names to mention.

This is mainly about the Cinque Terre, the most beautiful gem of this coastline. You will find here useful information about the five villages, what to see, what to do and what to eat, getting around, hiking trails, beaches, accommodation, tours and so much more. At the same time I show you what else is there to see in Eastern Liguria and give you some basic information about these coastal villages and towns. My recommendation is: book a room or apartment in one of the Cinque

Terre villages, and do some day trips from here to visit the beautiful Riviera di Levante.

And now, some basic information about the Cinque Terre. The Cinque Terre can be found in the eastern part of the Riviera di Levante, close to the border between Liguria and Tuscany. The name Cinque Terre literally means "Five lands", but in this case stands for "Five small medieval villages". These unique villages hide between green, steep hills and the turquoise Ligurian sea, their pastel-coloured houses are built on top of rocks or in little bays. When you look at them, you feel like you are in a fairy tale.

With 1,000 years of extremely hard work local people have turned the natural forests and rough, rocky, steep slopes into lush cultivated terraces. They have built about 7,000 kilometers of dry stone walls, carrying millions of baskets of stones and soil on their heads and shoulders, up and down the hills, climbing more than mountaineers. Once a terrace was ready, they planted vine, vegetables and basil, as well as different types of trees: mainly olive, lemon and orange.

The future of this unique landscape is however in danger. Young people often choose the easier way, they find a job in nearby cities, move away or make a living of local tourism. In the meantime, abandoned terraces collapse or are overtaken by maquis and forests. But luckily, there seems to be a new generation of enthusiastic young people who return to their roots. They follow the traditions of their grandparents, cultivate the land, make wine, limoncino, olive oil and pesto, and sell their products in the small alleyways. They are fantastic, passionate people who hopefully ensure the future of the Cinque Terre.

The Cinque Terre National Park is a great choice for an active holiday. You can hike on 100 kms of trails, swim in the tiny bays of this 15-km coastline, sea-kayak, dive, ride a bicycle, rent a boat, go fishing or sailing. You can do wine and olive oil tasting, take a pesto making or cooking course or sit around in one of the many restaurants and try the delicious local specialties.

Or if you prefer, just do nothing. It is a perfect place for slow travel. Read a newspaper while enjoying your morning espresso, learn some Italian phrases, walk around and get lost in the tiny back alleys, sleep on the beach once the crowds are gone, enjoy the orange sunset, feel the salty breeze from the sea, listen to the sound of the waves and cicadas, watch the old men playing bocce, enjoy an aperitivo in a nice little bar.

My perfect day in the Cinque Terre: wake up in Manarola, have breakfast on my terrace with sea view, hike my favourite Manarola-Volastra-Corniglia path, for lunch eat Alberto's focaccia in "La Gata Flora", in the afternoon swim and sunbathe in the hidden bay of Corniglia, admiring the colourful fish under the water, then return to Manarola by train. After a siesta go for dinner to the Trattoria dal Billy and ask for the recommended fresh fish of the day, accompanied by a bottle of Cinque Terre white wine. Later go for a night walk to the harbour and stop by to listen to some live music in La Cantina dello Zio Bramante. And of course, always take my camera with me.

The five villages

Riomaggiore

Riomaggiore is the most southern village of the Cinque Terre. It was first mentioned in the 13th century. The founders of the village moved from the hills to the sea, and built 3-4-storey houses on the rocky, steep territory. The houses have two entrances, one at the front, and one at the back, usually higher up. The buildings were constructed this way not only because of the steep hills, but also for safety reasons, so that the inhabitants could escape in case of Saracen attacks.

The village was built in the valley of the Rivus Maior (river), hence the name. The river was covered, it is now running under the main street. From the main street, Via Colombo, many sets of steps lead to small alleys further up the hill. The word "carruggio" refers to the tiny, narrow back alleys that you will find all around the Cinque Terre and Liguria. The houses are built close to one another, not much sun enters the back alleys, so they are nice and cool even during the hot summer months. Riomaggiore is like a labyrinth of alleys and steps, I still get lost once in a while. I don't mind it, I actually enjoy discovering new ways to get around.

Riomaggiore is divided into two by the railway line. The area by the sea with the colourful little boats (gozzi) and the drying nets is the fishing village (borgo dei pescatori) where tourists enjoy the mediterranean sun, local fishermen take a siesta, and you can watch a beautiful sunset from small seafood restaurants. The rocky beach of Riomaggiore can also be found around here, just take the trail to the left, along the sea.

Of course the fishermen work as well, at night or early morning, and many local traditional dishes are still based on the catch from the sea. From the main street, you can get to the fishing village through the underpass, following the "Marina" sign. This is one of my favourite spots in the Cinque Terre, I just can't get enough of the view of the colourful houses on top of one another. Looks best in the morning light.

The upper part is the agricultural village (borgo dei contadini), surrounded by terraces. This is where you'll find Via Colombo, the steep main street, with lot of steps on both sides. A simple walk around here is quite a workout! The main street is full of restaurants, bars and small shops. Above the railway lines a nice piazza was created, one of the few flat areas in the village. This is where kids are running around and playing soccer after school.

Further up, near the church runs Via Telemaco Signorini, named after the famous Italian impressionist painter. The Florence-born artist discovered Riomaggiore in 1860, then later returned several times, lived and worked in the village. He created beautiful paintings about the unique landscape and the life of the local people.

The main street and the railway station are connected by a long pedestrian tunnel. Pay attention to the nice mosaics! Near the station as well as on the walls of the Town Hall you will see the murals of an Italian-Argentinian artist named Silvio Benedetto. His interesting artworks are inspired by the hard work of local farmers.

Traditionally the famous coastal hiking path, the Sentiero Azzurro (Blue path) begins in Riomaggiore. The first section between Riomaggiore and Manarola is called Via dell'Amore (Lover's path). The path begins near the railway station with a set of steps; you will see the "Via dell'Amore" sign. Unfortunately the Via dell'Amore is currently closed because of a rock slide, and we don't know when it will be reopened. (UPDATE: A short section between the railway station of Manarola and the bar has been reopened.)

Last time I walked down the main street of Riomaggiore, I felt it was just too busy for me. Try to arrive early before the big groups arrive. If you are staying in the village, it's worth getting up early as this time of the day you will meet locals only. Get some fresh fruit and warm pastry for breakfast, and watch the fish vendor and the old ladies chatting in the street.

Quite a few seafood takeaway places popped up in Riomaggiore during the past years. Although I am a big fan of slow food, these can be good options if you just want a quick bite and something cheaper than restaurants. Try "Il Pescato Cucinato" or "Mamma Mia!". Riomaggiore is a good choice for young people who want to go out in the evening, sit around in bars and meet other travellers. Bar O'Netto and Vertical Bar are popular these days. Of course if you walk off the busy main street, you will find numerous wonderful, quiet little streets in Riomaggiore as well. I can offer accommodations in quiet places with great seaview, so Riomaggiore can also be a good base for discovering the Cinque Terre.

If you are looking for something nice to take home, look for my crazy and funny friend Oliver who has lived in Riomaggiore for about 10 years and is selling his own paintings of the villages. There are different size paintings, smaller ones as well, easy to take home as a gift. I have one on my wall and I love it! You can usually find him in the harbour of Riomaggiore or at Punta Bonfiglio in Manarola.

Cultural sights

Church of San Giovanni Battista
The church was built in 1340 but in 1870 the facade was rebuilt in a Neo-Gothic style. The Gothic doors on the right side, the rose window,

the wooden crucifix and the organ from 1851 are all well worth seeing. From the square in front of the church, you can enjoy a wonderful view of the village. I love walking up here at night, Riomaggiore is really pretty with the lights.

Castle
Not much is known about the castle that stands on top of the hill between the Rio Maggiore and the Rio Finale river valleys. According to historians, it was built in the second part of the 13th century for defence purposes. In case of attacks from the sea, the inhabitants were hiding here. During the 19th century, it was used as a cemetery. Today, it is a center for conferences, cultural events and weddings. The castle can be easily found if you follow the signs. Although you have to climb a few steps, the wonderful view is definitely worthwhile.

Oratory of San Rocco
The oratory can be found next to the castle. It was built in the 15th century in remembrance of the plague in the village.

Museo delle Cinque Terre Antiche Museum of local history
A museum about the origin and history of the Cinque Terre, the everyday life of locals, the real values of the area and why the Cinque Terre has become a UNESCO World Heritage site. (Currently closed.)

Manarola

Until a few years ago I had never heard of the Cinque Terre. Then one day a colleague of mine showed me an amazing photo of joyful, colourful houses on top of a huge rock rising from the sea. None of my friends knew this place, so it took us a long time to find out that the photo had been taken in Manarola, a tiny village by the Ligurian sea. Back then I did not think that soon I would know this place so well!

Manarola is even older than Riomaggiore, it was first mentioned in 1261. It is believed to have been founded by the inhabitants of Volastra, a village that existed already in Roman times. Volastra is located above Manarola, on top of the hill, and in Roman times travellers used to change horses here. The residents of Volastra farmed the surrounding terraces, planted olive, lemon and chestnut trees, as well as vines, then in the 12th century part of the population moved down to the sea and founded the village of Manarola. The name has a roman origin: it comes from a name of an altar dedicated to the Mani Gods, "manium arula". Other sources say that it derives from the words "magna roea", which means "a big mill wheel".

If you arrive on the path from Riomaggiore (currently closed), you will first see the back of the village. Once you get to the end of Via dell'Amore, you can descend to the railway station of Manarola. At the station you find a pedestrian tunnel, which will take you to the main street of Manarola. In the old days a creek used to run here and small bridges connected the two sides. In the upper part of the village you can still see the creek with some bridges. So when you exit the tunnel, turn right and walk all the way up to the square of the church (Piazza Papa Innocenzo IV) for an amazing view. Along the way you'll see an old mill wheel as well.

Once you pass the square, continue on the upper, quiet street of Manarola, Via Rollandi. You will also pass the best restaurant of Manarola, Trattoria dal Billy. At the end of the street you can return on Via Belvedere to the main street. Heading towards the sea from here, you will first come to Piazza Capellini. This piazza is not very old, it covers the railway lines, as trains used to rush through the middle of the village. On the other side of the square pay attention to the old photos.

I especially love the lower part of the main street, where fishing boats are parked just like cars in an average town. At the end you'll get to the harbour, which hides between two rocks. You can swim here, just jump off the rocks if you are brave enough or walk down the ladder. The water is deep, so for good swimmers only! The bay is full of fish, so take your snorkeling gear with you. This is one of my favourite spots for swimming. I love floating on my back and watching the colourful houses right above me, especially late afternoon when the colours are glowing. If you are lucky you can also watch how local fishermen pull up the boats from the sea with the crane.

Even though the Manarola-Corniglia coastal path is currently closed (to be opened soon), you should start walking towards Corniglia, to Punta Bonfiglio, as you can enjoy a breathtaking view of the village from the cemetery and the little park nearby. For kids there is a nice playground, for their parents there is a great bar called "Nessun Dorma". That's where the above mentioned photo was taken as well. Colours and lights are best here in the evening hours, before sunset.

Manarola along with Vernazza is registered among the most beautiful small villages of Italy (I borghi piú belli d'Italia). I'm not surprised. When I read an article about the Cinque Terre and there is one photo only, it is usually the well-known picture of Manarola.

Manarola is worth a visit during winter as well, as for the holiday season Mario Andreoli turns the hillside of Manarola into a huge nativity scene. The 300 characters are made of recycled materials, and are placed in a different way every year. Of course the nativity scene is the most beautiful at night, illuminated. You can see it from the start of December until the end of January. Different scenes are illuminated on August 10, the day of San Lorenzo, and at Easter time. It's possible to rent rooms with great views of the nativity scene.

Cultural sights

Church of San Lorenzo
The church, which was built in 1338, has a Gothic facade with a nice rose window, and a Baroque-style interior. On the facade, there is a

bas-relief representing the martyrdom of San Lorenzo. On the 15th-century triptych, you can see San Lorenzo with other saints. The church can be found in the upper part of the village. On the same square you will find a 14th-century oratory and a bell tower from the 13th century, originally built as a watch tower.

Bastion
Manarola's castle was probably built in the 13th century. Unfortunately, today, you can only see the remains of the bastion, surrounded by colourful houses.

Museo dello Sciacchetrá Sciacchetrá museum
In this museum, computer presentations, videos, photos and traditional objects will help you understand how this great dessert wine is made, and you can also learn about local life and the hard agricultural work on the terraces. (Currently closed.)

Corniglia

Corniglia is the smallest and quietest of the Cinque Terre villages. It is located 100 meters above sea level, on top of a small promontory. Houses are a bit different here, smaller and wider, similar to the houses of the villages inland.

I love the tiny Largo Taragio square in front of the oratory, it is very pleasant to relax at Bar Matteo in the shade of the trees and sunshades. Try the bruschetta (toast with chopped tomatoes mixed with garlic and basil) and the lemonade made from freshly picked lemons. Another nice little bar is "Pan e Vin" on Via Fieschi, run by a very friendly couple, Cristiana and Stefano. Stop by for coffee, a glass of wine or a sandwich. For delicious local produce in a relaxing atmosphere go to Km 0, just a few steps from Largo Taragio. If you are looking for something sweet, try the icecream at the Gelateria of Alberto. Best icecream in the Cinque Terre! If you are staying in Corniglia in an apartment with balcony, you can also buy nice local food in the little shops and have breakfast or dinner on your balcony while enjoying the seaview. There are more shops in Corniglia, my favourite is the "Alimentari Lisa" on the big square, right near the bus stop. Lisa is a very nice and friendly lady, and her prices are the best in Corniglia, so get your pesto, cheese and bottle of wine there.

The history of the village goes back to Roman times. According to the legend, Corniglia was founded by a wine producer, who named the village after his mother, Cornelia.

Corniglia doesn't have a harbour, so boats don't stop here. You can reach the village by car, train or foot. The railway station of Corniglia lies at sea level, there are different ways to get up to the center of the village. The most exciting version is climbing the Lardarina stairway with 382 steps. Once you get to the top, you will surely need that refreshing lemonade! You can also walk up to the center along the winding paved road, I think it is easier. Walking from the station towards Corniglia, you will see a sign: stairs to the left, road to the right. Of course, there is also an easy option: the local electronic buses regularly run between the station and the center. However, the last bus leaves around 7.30PM so in the evening you surely have to walk.

After catching your breath at the top of the steps, start walking to the left and you will get to a square. From here, just follow the "Centro" sign to the left into the small street (Via Fieschi) and you will find yourself on the main square of Corniglia (Largo Taragio). You can find a small fountain on the wall under the oratory; make sure you refill your bottles here. Kids play soccer behind the oratory, the gate is painted on the back of the building. This is the cutest soccer field I've ever seen, with az amazing view of the sea and Manarola. Continue walking down Via Fieschi to the panorama terrace from where you can admire the entire Cinque Terre coast. A new bar opened on this terrace, Bar Terza Terra, so you can enjoy an aperitivo while watching the sunset.

It's worth walking up to the cemetery as well, as it is quite different than in other countries, with a breathtaking panorama. The small bench hidden behind the cemetery is probably the quietest spot of the village, perfect for some romantic moments.

Because of its location many believe that Corniglia does not have a beach. Well, they are wrong, there are actually 3 beaches around here. I prefer the hidden little bay behind and below the village. You can reach it following the Marina sign. No surprise, more steps are coming! This marina is never too crowded, the water is beautiful and clean, but it is also deep, so for good swimmers only.

Cultural sights

Church of San Pietro

The 14th-century church is one of the most interesting monuments of the Ligurian Gothic style. The rose window on the facade is made of white Carrara marble and it has Corniglia's ancient symbol, a deer, in the middle. Make sure you walk inside as well, you will see a 12th-century christening font and a polyptych.

Oratory of the Disciplinati of Santa Caterina

The 18th-century monument stands above the Largo Taragio square. You can enjoy a beautiful view from behind the oratory.

Vernazza

Vernazza is the pearl of the Cinque Terre, simply breathtaking. Unfortunately it is packed with tourists but mornings and evenings are quieter and low season months are very pleasant. Vernazza along with Manarola is registered among the most beautiful small villages of Italy (I borghi piú belli d'Italia).

No one knows exactly where the name Vernazza comes from. It might have been named after the Vernaccia wine.

Vernazza was the only village with a natural harbour so ships departed from here to the Republic of Genoa and other countries. As a result,

Vernazza was the most prosperous village with economical and political power. This wealth is shown even today by beautiful arcades, archways and balconies. In medieval times there was no main square, beach or breakwater, the waves were splashing at the houses. Boats were also moored to the walls, so Vernazza was a bit like Venice.

The backbone of the village is the main street; smaller streets (carruggi) run parallel with it. The main street runs to the main square (Piazza Marconi), this is the center, the heart of the village, the "gossip corner", with several bars and restaurants, colourful houses, drying clothes, boats, piles of fishing nets and lazy cats. Just by the piazza, there is a small sandy beach and a harbour.

After a strenuous hike in the summer, I usually can't wait to jump into the water. If you are a good swimmer, go to the end of the pier and dive into the water, or simply walk down the ladder. It's a fabulous experience to swim around the colourful fishing boats, with the magnificent piazza in the background. There are fewer people here and the water is cleaner. Of course, if you are with kids, it is better to bathe at the sandy beach. In the harbour, locals often play waterpolo. In the 1970s, the waterpolo team of Vernazza was among the best.

The view of Vernazza is determined by the defense system which was built by the Genoan people to protect Vernazza against Saracens, barbarian tribes and pirate attacks. Castles and bastions have been reinforced several times, their remains can still be seen today.

In my opinion you have to see Vernazza at least from 4 different points. Every view is different and stunning!

1. From the path, as you arrive from Corniglia.

2. From the path, as you start walking towards Monterosso. Once you have walked up many steps and are high enough, don't forget to look back. From this point, you can enjoy one of the most beautiful sceneries of the Cinque Terre. (I think it is worth hiking up here even if you don't go all the way to Monterosso.) The bastion, the belltower and the pier wonderfully surround the small harbour, the turquoise water and the colourful fishing boats.

3. From the end of the pier, with the colourful boats in the foreground and the houses of the main square in the background.

4. From the tower of the Doria castle.

During the horrible flood of October 25, 2011 Vernazza was devastated. The town was buried in mud and rocks, the ground floor basically disappeared. Homes and businesses were ruined. Thanks to the incredibly hard work of local people and all the help received from outside, Vernazza is beautiful as ever. However, you can still see some signs of the disaster. Probably the only advantage of the flood is a new rocky beach, created by the power of nature. You can reach it from the main street, crossing a small tunnel.

Cultural sights

Church of Santa Margarita d'Antiochia

The church, which stands on the main square of Vernazza, was constructed in 1318 in Ligurian Gothic style. Its belltower is 40 meters high and has an octogonal shape. At an open-air art festival, there was a rope connecting the belltower with a temporary tower on the other side of the beach. As part of the show, the belltower went up in flames and a rope dancer escaped, walking on the rope high above the little harbour. It was an amazing experience!

Doria castle and Belforte tower

The round tower of the castle of this Genoan noble family is still an important building in Vernazza. From the Belforte tower, you can enjoy a magnificent view of the village and its colourful harbour

Monterosso al Mare

To be honest, for me Monterosso is the least exciting of the 5 villages. It is a bit more like an "average" summer resort with its long beach and several hotels. However, if you are an elderly person or travelling with kids, this might be the most comfortable village for you: there are less stairs, most of the area is flat and it is easier to get to the parking or the railway station. This village awaits tourists with a nice long beach, deck-chairs and umbrellas, hotels and some night life. Unfortunately you have to pay on most of the beach but there are some free areas: in front of the railway station, under the statue of the

Giant and at the end of the beach towards Vernazza, near the historical center.

The promenade is very nice with oleanders, bougainvilleas and palm trees. Locals bike around, which would be impossible in the other villages. In 2006, Forbes Traveler listed Monterosso among the 25 sexiest beaches of the world, along with Hawaii, Mexico and the Maldives. This award goes not only to the beach of Monterosso but to the entire beauty of the Cinque Terre National Park and the five unique villages.

The history of Monterosso dates back to 643 when the people living in the hills moved down to the sea, hiding from barbarian tribes. The village is named Monterosso because the ruling family used to have red hair. "Monte dei rossi" means "Mountain of the ginger-haired".

The historical center of Monterosso has a really nice atmosphere with many small streets, pastel-coloured houses and artisan shops. The main square - Piazza Garibaldi - hosts the town hall and the statue of Garibaldi. If you walk a bit further towards Vernazza, you will see old men playing bocce, a traditional game with balls.

The old town and the new, modern area (Fegina) are separated by the San Cristoforo hill and are connected by a pedestrian tunnel. For a nicer experience walk along the sea, avoiding the tunnel. For the best view hike up the San Cristoforo hill, and admire the entire Cinque

Terre coastline. Once you are on top, spend some time there, visit the Convent of Cappuccini, the Church of San Francesco and the cemetery.

As Monterosso was often under attacks by pirates and other enemies, a strong defense system was built to protect the village. In the 16th century, guards kept an eye on the sea from 13 watchtowers. Luckily you can still see the remains of the castle, the city wall, a watchtower and the Aurora tower.

Monterosso offers a little more nightlife than the other 4 villages, but do not expect loud party places and bars that are open until next morning. You can enjoy wonderful dinners and sit around drinking wine until late at night, but if you want to go out dancing every night, you'd better stay in Viareggio.

Cultural sights

Statue of the Giant - Il Gigante
The statue of the Giant can be found between Fegina beach and the small harbour. The Giant is actually Neptune, the god of the sea and he is holding the terrace of an old villa on his shoulders. The 14-meter tall statue was made in 1910 by sculptor Arrigo Minerbi and an architect named Levacher. The statue was badly damaged by the powerful sea storm in 1966. According to plan, the Argentinian artist Silvio Benedetto will restore the monumen

The "Yellow pagoda"

There is a house not far from the Giant where Eugenio Montale, Nobel-prize winner Italian poet, used to spend his summer holidays. The villages of the Cinque Terre inspired many of his poems. Locals call the house "yellow pagoda".

Convent of Cappuccini and Church of San Francesco
The convent with the church can be found on top of the San Cristoforo hill. It was built in 1619 and during the centuries it was used as hospital and warehouse as well until it was returned to its rightful owners. Among other artwork, you can also see Van Dyck's Crucifixion inside. Next to the church, you will find the cemetery.

Church of San Giovanni Battista
The 13th-century church is located in the historical center of Monterosso, and is another nice example of Ligurian Gothic style. Its beautiful facade is comprised of alternating strips of white marble and green serpentine. Its belltower was originally part of Monterosso's defence system, used as a watch tower. The Baroque altar dates back to 1744.

Oratory of Confraternita dei Neri
The 16th-century Baroque oratory can be found in the old town of Monterosso, near the church of San Giovanni Battista.

Oratory of Confraternita dei Bianchi, Santa Croce
This oratory is located in the old town of Monterosso as well, behind the church of San Giovanni Battista. So within a few steps you can see

three interesting sights. You should spend some time inside the oratory as well, the 19th-century organ is well worth seeing.

Aurora tower
The 16th-century Aurora tower is located by the sea, at the foot of the hill of the Cappuccini. This tower is fortunately in good condition.

Centro de salagione delle acciughe Anchovy salting center
You can learn everything about anchovies and how they get from the sea to your plate. You can also do some tasting and buy a jar or two. When I visited the center, they had a black and white film on DVD, which showed life in the Cinque Terre in the 1940s. Very interesting, so worth having a look!

Travel and Tourism

Destinations

Groppo

Groppo is a tiny hamlet between Manarola and Volastra. You will drive by if you arrive by car on the coastal road (parking is free), or you can take the small bus from Manarola. For the best experience, hike here from Manarola or Volastra.

There are only a few colourful houses here, so you can quickly discover the village. It's really quiet, so come up here if you feel you have met too many tourists at the seaside railway stations.

The Cinque Terre Wine Cooperative can be found in Groppo as well; that's where most of the Cinque Terre wine is made. Stop by in their shop (by the road); it's full of delicious local products and souvenirs.

Just below the village you can also find an old olive mill, but it's closed at the moment.

Volastra

Volastra can be found above Manarola, on top of a hill. It looks like it stands on a green terrace with seaview. The houses were built in a semicircular form, in line with the surrounding cultivated terraces. In the old days, this construction method helped to protect the settlements; there are many similar villages in Liguria.

The name Volastra comes from the expression "Vicus Oleaster", which means "the village of the olive". Later it became Oleastra, then Volastra. The origin of the name is not surprising, as Volastra lies in the middle of beautiful olive groves. Most of the Cinque Terre olive oils come from this area.

Volastra has basically 2 streets, so you can quickly walk around it. The main attraction is the medieval Nostra Signora della Salute church, which was first mentioned in 1240. I just love these tiny village churches, they touch my soul more than a huge baroque basilica. It's a great place for some quiet moments.

The local festival takes place on August 5.

Volastra plays an important role in the history of the Cinque Terre, as Manarola was founded by the inhabitants of Volastra when they moved down to the sea from the hills.

Volastra is located by the wonderful Cinque Terre panorama road, so you can easily reach it by car. Parking is free. You can also take the small local bus from Manarola which runs several times during the day. But my suggestion is to arrive on foot, from Manarola or from Corniglia, as one of the most beautiful hiking trails of the Cinque Terre runs through Volastra.

You will find a couple of fountains here to refill your water bottle, also a small store and a restaurant. (Usually closed during siesta hours.)

San Bernardino

The hamlet of San Bernardino can be found above Corniglia. It is worth a visit for its tranquility and one of the best views in the Cinque Terre. You can drive or walk up here. (Parking is free.) There is also a local bus service from Corniglia a couple of times a day.

The village is located along a ridge. At one end of the village, you will find the small church of San Bernardino. From the bench near the church, you can enjoy a breathtaking view of Corniglia, Manarola and the turquoiseGuvano bay. Take some time to relax here, under the huge fig tree.

The village has only a few inhabitants. There is a small bar where local old men play cards, read their newspapers and just enjoy retired life. The bar which is also a small shop is run by Signora Franca, who is a very kind lady.

You will see the sign "Basso" in several places, as almost all the families who live here are called Basso. San Bernardino is also named the village of the Basso.

Gulf of the Poets

La Spezia

La Spezia is a city close to the Cinque Terre. If you are driving from Rome, Tuscany or Venice, you have to drive through La Spezia to get to the Cinque Terre coastal road. If you are taking the train, you'll probably change trains at La Spezia Centrale station. The to the Cinque Terre also depart from La Spezia.

The city is quite big, with about 100,000 inhabitants. It has a beautiful location in the Gulf of La Spezia surrounded by green hills and with the view of the mountains in the background. It has one of the main Italian harbours and also the arsenal of the Italian Navy can be found here. La Spezia is a pleasant city, if you spend a longer holiday in the area, it's worth a visit. I actually like it because it is not a touristy place like Rome, Florence or Venice, although it has a castle, some churches, museums and nice Art Nouveau-style villas. I'd say it is an average Italian town with mainly local people around and everyday life going on. So it's actually fun to experience it. Instead of souvenir shops, you will find here stores for the inhabitants, so it's the perfect place to shop for clothes, shoes, books, Italian music CDs, etc.

What you surely should not miss is the local market. I just love this market. Besides fruits and vegetables, you can buy delicious local stuff: pesto, cheese, ham, olives, artichoke, anchovies, jam, honey, etc. There is also an important fish market here. I always buy the 5-liter box of wonderful ligurian olive oil here which comes from the nearby olive mill featured in our olive harvest video. If you are staying in a Cinque Terre apartment for several days, you should come here on your first day and do your food shopping, it is much cheaper than the village shops. Just to give you an example, 1 kg of pesto costs around 16 EUR here while you pay 48 EUR for the same in the Cinque Terre. The market is open every day except Sunday between 7AM and 1PM. If you enjoy good food and cooking, check out the "Cooking course with market visit" tour on the site, it takes place in La Spezia.

Another good place to visit is the harbour of La Spezia. There is a nice promenade along the sea with flowers, palm trees and nice villas. Cross the new modern bridge to Porto Mirabello, the harbour for super yachts. You can admire the luxury yachts, walk around in the shopping center, have a drink in one of the bars or relax in the beautifully located and expensive swimming pool. If you only come for a day, you can park your car here and take the boat to the Cinque Terre, Portovenere and Lerici. The Cinque Terre sailing tour that I recommend also starts from the port of La Spezia.

If you arrive with a cruise ship and only have a short day to visit the Cinque Terre, I can help you to make the most of your day, and offer you a local guide and private transport if necessary. If you arrive by car for a day, just park your car in La Spezia and take the train: Riomaggiore is only 9 minutes away. If you want, you can buy the Cinque Terre card at the station and there is also a National Park information office here. If you are travelling by train and only do a day trip to the Cinque Terre, you can leave your bags at the luggage deposit of La Spezia Centrale station.

You can even choose La Spezia as your home for your holiday, there are beautiful apartments for rent. Driving to La Spezia is not an issue, and you can easily reach from here not only the Cinque Terre, but also Portovenere, Lerici, Tellaro as well as other beautiful places in Liguria and Tuscany.

Le Grazie

I'd like to quickly mention Le Grazie, a pretty seaside town between La Spezia and Portovenere, in the Gulf of La Spezia. I had travelled through it several times by bus on my way to Portovenere but I never really paid attention. Then one day, we were driving to the Festa della Madonna Bianca in Portovenere. We arrived early afternoon, and by that time all the parking places in Portovenere were full. So we had to turn around and drive all the way back to Le Grazie. Luckily, we found parking there and decided to take a short walk.

It was a nice surprise, a very pleasant, quiet seaside town with a beautiful harbour nestled between green hills: colourful fishing and sailing boats, a small beach, cute little cafes, and a good icecream shop which we tried right away. Le Grazie is really worth a stop on your way to Portovenere, if you are driving or taking the bus from La Spezia.

Portovenere and the 3 islands

If Riomaggiore is the first village of the Cinque Terre, Portovenere could be village "zero". Although it is officially not part of the Cinque Terre, it is well worth a visit.

Portovenere sits on a rocky peninsula in the Gulf of Poets. It was once popular with poets and writers such as Byron, Shelley and Lawrence. With its small harbour lined with colourful houses, its narrow streets leading up to the castle and the church standing on top of the rock, Portovenere is one of my favourite places to visit.

Portovenere was first mentioned in 161 A.D. as "Portus Veneris"; the Romans used it as a naval station. After 1113, Portovenere belonged to the Republic of Genoa and became an important marine base. In 1160 the construction of the city wall and the castle started. The promontory is dominated by the 13th century Church of San Pietro.

There are several ways to get to Portovenere from the villages of the Cinque Terre:

Portovenere can be reached by boat which runs during the day between Portovenere, La Spezia and the Cinque Terre villages. When you arrive from the sea, you will first see the church of San Pietro sitting on top of the rock, which is quite an incredible view. I think this is the best way to travel here, unless you want to hike.

You can reach Portovenere by car but of course you cannot enter the historical center. You can park close to the harbour but during the main season it can be hard to find a parking space.

You can take a train to La Spezia, then take a bus to Portovenere. Unfortunately the bus does not leave from the railway station, you have to walk about 15 minutes to the bus stop. As you leave the building of the railway station, you have to start walking to the left until Piazza Garibaldi. Turn right there, walk straight down Viale Garibaldi. The bus stop can be found next to the Arsenale.

You can hike from Riomaggiore on trail 3 or 3a until the Telegrafo, then on trail 1 until Portovenere. It is not an easy hike but there will be no crowds and the views are simply breathtaking!

When you arrive to Portovenere, you will enter the historical center through the city gate. On the right side, you will see the remains of the city wall, which run up to the castle. As you walk down the main street

(Via G. Capellini), you can admire medieval houses and turn into small shops. At the end of this carruggio, you will find the Church of San Pietro. From here you can enjoy an amazing view of the sea and the rocky coastline. Byron's Cave can be found here as well; this is where the famous poet used to swim. On your way back, start walking up the steps and you will reach the Church of San Lorenzo. From here you can climb up to the castle. After you have visited the village, enjoy a nice meal in one of the restaurants of the harbour.

There are 3 small islands close to Portovenere - Palmaria, Tino and Tinetto - which together with Portovenere are a UNESCO World Heritage site. There are excursion boats leaving from the harbour that go around the islands.

Palmaria is the biggest island with beautiful beaches. It is accessible by ferry or water taxi. The highlight of the island is the Blue Grotto which you can reach only from the sea. There is also a nice hiking trail around the island, offering fantastic views of Portovenere.

Tino is currently a military zone, it is open to the public only on September 13, the day of San Venerio. The ruins of the 11th century San Venerio abbey can be found here.

Tinetto is just a bigger rock and is also a military zone. It holds the ruins of a 6th century monastery.

If you can, come to Portovenere on August 17th. It is the day of the Festa della Madonna Bianca, my favourite festival in the area.

Cultural sights

Church of San Pietro
This church was constructed in 1277 over the ruins of another church dedicated to Venus. Venus is Venere in Italian, while Porto means harbour, so that's where the name of the town comes from. The Genoan-Gothic building is beautiful with its black and white stripes, perched on top of a rock in the sea. Next to the church, don't miss the Romanesque style arcades with amazing view towards the Cinque Terre.

Church of San Lorenzo
The Romanesque style church was built in the 12th century. Unfortunately, it was badly damaged during the centuries and had to be rebuilt several times.

Andrea Doria castle
The castle, which took the Genoan centuries (12-17.) to build, dominates the town of Portovenere. Several towers of the local defence system are still in good condition. From the castle, you can enjoy a fantastic view over the St. Peter church and the sea.

Harbour
Several excursion and fishing boats are anchored in the harbour, and you will find several bars and restaurants around there. The tall

colourful houses (palazzata) used to be part of the medieval defense system.

Tramonti

I just love Tramonti. It's a breathtaking, wild area between Riomaggiore and Portovenere with clusters of houses along the coast: Persico, Schiara, Monesteroli, Fossola, Campi and Canetto. There are several "off the beaten track" hiking trails around here, offering you amazing views.

You can hike here from Riomaggiore, taking trail number 3 to Telegrafo, trail number 1 to Sant' Antonio, then choosing between the different paths to go to Fossola, Monesteroli or Schiara. If you have a car, you can drive a bit closer, then do shorter walks. If you are coming from Riomaggiore, just before the long tunnel, on the right side of the road, you will see the information center and shop of the Cinque Terre National Park. If you park your car there, you can easily walk down to Casotti and Fossola. The church of Fossola is very pretty with the view of Monesteroli in the background. Path 4/b takes you from Fossola to the famous Monesteroli steps (see large photo at the top) but last time we were there (in 2014) it was closed at one point, and I am not sure what the current situation is. If it is closed, you have to walk up the steps to Sant' Antonio, then down to Monesteroli. Expect many steps taking you almost down to the sea, and don't forget, you'll also have to walk up. It's a wonderful experience, but I don't recommend it if you are suffering from vertigo.

If you prefer, you can drive all the way to Sant' Antonio. Coming from Riomaggiore, after the long tunnel, there is a road to the left, towards Biassa, Telegrafo and Sant' Antonio. At Sant' Antonio, you will also find a gym in the forest, the "Palestra nel Verde", just in case the steps don't make you tired enough. I personally had enough of a workout hiking around so instead of the "green gym", I headed to the nice open air bar for a huge ham and cheese focaccia sandwich and a glass of wine.

You can also drive to Campiglia and hike from there. In this case, you will see Schiara first. All the houses in the area were built by farmers from Campiglia and Biassa, and were used as cellars, storehouses and holiday houses in the season. For many years, the area was abandoned but people started to buy and renovate the houses, and use them as holiday homes. Needless to say, these holiday houses are not for the lazy ones. We met a man who gave up city life and lives here all year long with his mum. His children and friends often come to visit of course. I am quite jealous of the garden and the view he has... We met him on the trail and he was really friendly, he invited us right away for a glass of wine on his terrace.

Below Schiara, you can see the Scoglio Ferale (the Ferale rock). On top of the rock, there is a white cross, in memory of Luigi Garavaglio, who was a navy topographer and died in 1911 falling from the rock during his work. The rock looks really nice in the sea with the colourful flowers of Tramonti in the foreground.

Lerici

Lerici is located on the east side of the Gulf of Poets, opposite to Portovenere. It's a very pretty seaside town with a beautiful promenade, a harbour with fishing and sailing boats, a large piazza with several bars and restaurants, tiny alleyways in the old town and an imposing castle. For centuries, this beautiful area has inspired international and Italian artists. The poet Shelley and his wife Mary Shelley also lived in Lerici in 1822. Shelley actually died here during a tempest.

Although close to Tuscany and the Cinque Terre, foreign tourists don't really know Lerici. On the other hand, it's a popular holiday destination among North Italian families. The beaches around Lerici are packed in July and August but the town is fairly quiet during the rest of the year.

The 13th-century Pisan Castle dominates the view of Lerici. If you walk up there, you will enjoy a nice panorama overlooking the town and the harbour. When I was climbing up to the castle, I met a nice lady who was 100 years old! She still went for a little walk every day which was quite a workout as her house was on a steep street. I guess those steps and of course living in this beautiful part of the world kept her healthy for that long.

You can drive to Lerici, arrive by bus from La Spezia or take the boat from Portovenere. There are beautiful beaches around here so make sure you bring your swimsuit with you. Once you are in Lerici, you should definitely visit Tellaro as well; it's walking distance but you can also take the bus

Tellaro

Some friends of mine who saw my photos of Tellaro thought it was one of the Cinque Terre villages. Well, yes, it's another picture-perfect village, a real gem hidden at the end of Liguria, close to the tuscan border. A charming, romantic place in the Gulf of Poets with bright houses, colourful fishing boats, a cute church and quiet, narrow alleyways. Tellaro is registered among the most beautiful villages of Italy (I borghi piú belli d'Italia).

You can drive here if you have a car or take the bus from La Spezia. I actually took the bus from La Spezia to **Lerici**, then walked from Lerici to Tellaro and in the evening took the bus from Tellaro to La Spezia. It is a beautiful and easy walk, and you will even pass a wonderful beach, so make sure you take your swimsuit with you. Once you are in Tellaro, enjoy the great views from the main square or from the lookout point near the Oratory of San Maria in Selaa and take time to walk around in the small passages. Of course, my favourite part of the village is the small piazza with the colourful fishing boats and the rose coloured, 16th-century Church of San Giorgio.

There are also several hiking trails in the area. A good choice can be a walk to Montemarcello which is another pretty village with nice views of Portovenere and the islands on the other side. Of course, if you have a car, you can also drive to Montemarcello.

I think if you look at the photos in the gallery, you will understand why I love this place. If you have more than a couple of days in the Cinque Terre, you should definitely visit Tellaro as well. You could do a Lerici-Tellaro-Portovenere day trip, there is also a boat service between Lerici and Portovenere. But check the timetables in advance, as these boats run only a few times a day.

On the way to Genova

Levanto

Levanto could be the 6th village of the Cinque Terre, it can be found after Monterosso, on the other side of Punta Mesco. It is a very pleasant town with a long beach (sand and pebbles). Levanto is a perfect base for discovering the Cinque Terre which is only 5 minutes away by train but you can also reach it by boat from Levanto. If you hike up the hill, you will find Monterosso on the other side. It is a very picturesque, 2-hour hike.

The town centre has a very nice atmosphere. You will notice that the buildings are different here to those of the Cinque Terre villages. Windows, balconies are painted on the walls; they look almost real from a distance. (Trompe l'oeil) This shows that Levanto was always richer than the Cinque Terre villages. You can find several nice restaurants and little shops in town, as well as a good covered market, a great place to buy local produce. Every Wednesday, there is also a small street market selling clothes, games, kitchen utensils and all kinds of stuff. Piazza Cavour is the main square and there is even a tiny cinema hiding nearby: only for Italian speakers, as every movie is dubbed in Italy.

Interesting to know that there are 22 tiny villages scattered around the Levanto Valley, which belong to Levanto. Some of them only consist of a few houses built around a nice little church or chapel with a wonderful hilltop location. If you have the time and a car, drive around and visit some of these villages.

Try to be in Levanto on July 25th as there is a huge festival in town! This is the day of San Giacomo, the local patron saint.

The history of Levanto dates back to the Romans. From the 13th century, the settlement belonged to the Republic of Genoa but it could keep its independence and it was a wealthy trading town. Even today people live well here but in the 21st century the main source of income is tourism. Even the famous Fiat-owner Agnelli family has a huge holiday estate here. You will find the beautiful villas and the large garden at the far end of the beach, towards Monterosso.

Everyone is riding a bike around Levanto so you should also do that. There are two good bike-rental shops in town, but I personally like Fabio's "Sensafreni Bike Shop" on Piazza del Popolo. Once you have cycled around the streets of Levanto, try the fantastic bicycle path along the sea.

Cultural sights

Church of Sant Andrea
The 13th-century church is a nice example of Ligurian Gothic style. Its facade is comprised of alternating white and dark green strips with a white marble rose window.

Castle and Clock Tower
If you start walking up the hill towards Monterosso, you will find a nice historical area. The castle was built by the Malaspina family in the 11th century then later rebuilt by the Genoan people. For a long time it served as a prison, today it is a private residence. The Clock Tower dates back to 1265. You can also see the remains of the medieval city walls.

Medieval loggia
There is a pretty square close to the sea, Piazza del Popolo, with a medieval loggia from 1405. When it was constructed, it was unique in all of Liguria.

Bonassola

Bonassola is a tranquil seaside town with a long sandy/pebbled beach. It gets very busy in August, full of North Italian families, but nice and quiet during the rest of the year. The beach is great for kids as well.

If you are spending several days in the Cinque Terre, come to Bonassola for a day. You can drive here or take the train, but my recommendation is to arrive by bike, on the Levanto-Bonassola-Framura bicycle path. The EBike tour is also a great way to visit Bonassola.

Bonassola is great for swimming and walking around but if you want culture, you will also find several churches and a 16th-century castle here. The most famous sight of Bonassola is probably the Madonnina della Punta, a tiny church built at the end of the promontory, to the right of the beach. It's a great panorama point, you can see all the way to the Cinque Terre to the left, and the Portofino peninsula to the right. If you get hungry, I recommend the focaccia on the lovely square close to the beach.

Framura

Framura is a very interesting village, it has more levels. You don't meet many people here so it's a great place if you would like to hide away a bit from the world. We visited Framura in August, in the middle of the tourist season, but didn't really meet anyone apart from the kids playing basketball in the small street. Of course, there were more people on Framura's beaches.

You can arrive by car or train but it's more fun to bike here on the Levanto-Bonassola-Framura bicycle path. The EBike tour is also a great way to see Framura.

If you come by bike or train, you will arrive at the lowest part of the village, down by the sea. Here you will find a nice harbour full of colourful boats and a bar, which is open only during the season. If you want to get to the highest part of the village, be prepared for a nice climb! Framura is made of 5 smaller parts (so called *frazione*): Anzo, Castagnola, Costa, Ravecca and Setta. The higher you get, the better the view of course. In Framura, I saw a store, a bar and a pizzeria but all were closed during the siesta hours so if you'd like to have lunch here, make sure you come around noon.

There are several beaches around the village. "Porto Pidocchio" bay is easy to reach, right from the bike path, before getting to Framura. At the very end of the path, you can find another bike rental place.

Deiva Marina

Deiva Marina is a peaceful seaside resort between the Cinque Terre and Genoa. It has a nice long sandy beach which is quite rare in this part of Liguria. It is an ideal place for families with small kids. If you stay in the Cinque Terre and want to spend a day with your children swimming, sunbathing and building sand castles, take the train to Deiva Marina, it's just a few stops away.

People might say there is not a lot to do in Deiva Marina. That's why it's a great place! Not many shops, not many bars and not many tourists. It's just a perfect place for a relaxing day. You can spend the whole day on the beach, but it's actually worth taking a nice walk around the old town. This area dates back to the 9th century and has colourful houses and narrow alleyways just like the other towns mentioned on this homepage. The old town is actually on the other side of Deiva Marina, close to the hills. The area near the sea is new and modern with hotels, restaurants and gift shops.

There is also a cute street market here Saturday mornings, so if you are staying in an apartment and need some cheese, ham and wine, this is a good place to buy it.

There are several hiking trails in the area, you can walk to Framura, Bonassola or Moneglia on the other side.

Moneglia

Moneglia lies in a beautiful bay between the two promontories of Punta Moneglia and Punta Rospo. It is another great choice for families with small kids as it has a nice sandy beach, protected by breakwater. The beach is also awarded with the Blue Flag. The town is surrounded by huge olive groves so Moneglia is also famous for its extra virgin olive oil. Local focaccia and olive oil can be tasted at the Olive Oil Fair which is held yearly on Easter Monday.

You can easily reach Moneglia by car or train, or you can even hike here from neighbouring villages. There are several beautiful walking paths in the area offering you amazing seaviews. If you come with kids, you'll probably spend most of the day on the sandy beach, otherwise make sure you spend some time discovering this pretty town.

There are wonderful little streets with colourful medieval houses, artisan shops, nice restaurants and two churches (Church of San Giorgio and Church of Santa Croce). The Church of San Giorgio also has a Franciscan cloister; I really love its beautiful courtyard.

You can also visit the 12th-century Castle of Monleone and the Fortress of Villafranca. I really enjoyed the view of Moneglia from the Fortress of Villafranca. From here, you can see the castle and both bell towers. The fortress is surrounded by a nice mediterranean garden.

Sestri Levante

I don't have stunning photos of Sestri Levante; every time I went there, it was cloudy and grey. However, this should not discourage you from visiting this picturesque ligurian town. Sestri Levante is actually quite big with close to 20,000 inhabitants but you should concentrate on the old part on the peninsula.

From the railway station head towards the sea. You will soon find yourself on Via XXV Aprile with cute little stores and seafood restaurants. This main street runs towards the end of the promontory and if you turn left or right, you will get to one of the famous bays of Sestri Levante: Baia del Silenzio (Bay of Silence) to the east, and Baia delle Favole (Bay of Fables) to the west. The Baia delle Favole was named in honour of the Danish writer Hans Christian Andersen who lived in Sestri for a while in 1833.

I've just read a list of the most beautiful beaches of Italy, chosen by Italians. Baia del Silenzio was on the list as the only beach from Liguria. I don't quite agree; in my opinion there are some more beautiful beaches in Liguria but this bay is surely one of the most famous ones among Italians. And yes, it is very pretty with the colourful houses and its sandy beach. It is also a favourite spot of local people. When the water is too cold for swimming, they are just having a picnic or playing ball games with the kids. Baia delle Favole is bigger, with a long sandy beach and a nice promenade.

If you enjoy hiking, don't miss the trail to Punta Manara. Look for the sign on the left side of Via XXV Aprile as you are walking towards the old town. It's a very nice hike, mainly up on the way there. From the viewpoints, you will enjoy the most magnificent view of the promontory and the Baia del Silenzio.

Portofino peninsula

Santa Margherita Ligure

Santa Margherita Ligure is a good starting point for a beautiful daytrip around the Portofino peninsula. My recommendation is: take an early train to Santa Margherita Ligure, hike or take the boat following the Santa Margherita Ligure-Portofino-San Fruttuoso-Camogli circle, then take the train back to your accommodation from Camogli. The peninsula is full of wonderful hiking trails but unless you are a very fit and experienced hiker, it's better to hike one or two sections, and for the rest of the trip, take the boat.

When you get off the train at Santa Margherita Ligure railway station, watch carefully your belongings. I am not sure what the current situation is but for years there was a group (including women and kids) focusing on tourists, causing some chaos as people were trying to get on and off trains with their luggage and stealing their valuables. So be careful there. Once you walk out of the station, go down the stairway, this will take you to the beach and the center of town.

Santa Margherita Ligure is an old fashioned riviera resort with elegant (and mostly expensive) hotels, restaurants and shops. There are many beaches in and around town, mainly private beaches, but you will also find free public ones. Make sure you have your swimming suit with you. In the center, you can enjoy walking around narrow streets between beautifully restored houses, then head down to the harbour which is full of yachts and fishing boats. In the park by the water, you will see two interesting monuments: the Statue of Cristoforo Colombo, who was born in the area, and the Statue of Vittorio Emanuele II, the first king of united Italy.

The hills around the bay are full of amazing villas, hiding in nice Italian gardens. (I wonder how many million euros they cost... not that I am planning to buy.) There is also a villa and garden that you can visit, the 17th-century Villa Durazzo and its public gardens. It's nice to sit around here for a while and enjoy the magnificent panorama of the coast.

If you are on a budget, make a sandwich in your apartment or grab some stuff for a picnic in Santa Margherita Ligure. Portofino and San Fruttuoso restaurants are not cheap.

Once you have looked around Santa Margherita, take the boat to Portofino, or you can also take the bus. If you choose to hike this section, you have two choices. You can follow the trail over the hills or just walk on the pavement along the sea which is the easier version. I love both. By the sea, you will see more breathtaking villas and there are many small beaches with crystal clear water so you can combine walking and swimming. If you have snorkeling equipment, take it with you, as there are lot of fish in this protected marine area.

Portofino

As I wrote on the Santa Margherita Ligure page, the best way to get to Portofino is from Santa Margherita Ligure. You can drive but I don't recommend it. Portofino is very small with limited parking so most of the time you cannot even enter the village. Instead, you can take the bus or the boat but the best is to walk there. There is a hiking trail with some ups and downs or you can just follow the road along the sea for a flat and easy walk. You will pass cute little bays perfect for a quick, refreshing swim. There are also some great sights on the way. First, I would like to mention the Cervara Abbey (Abbazia). It has a beautiful Italian garden with seaview. As my husband is a passionate gardener, we had to visit of course. Timing is an important issue here, visits are allowed on every first and third Sunday of the month, from March to October.

Not long after passing the Abbey, you will get to a breathtaking turquoise bay, Paraggi. You just have to go for a swim here! Irresistible. The beach itself is very crowded during the summer. Most of it is private but there is a narrow free section in the middle. Here is my tip: as you walk towards Portofino and first see the Paraggi bay after the big bend to the right, you will see some steps on the left side. It takes you down to a rocky area with a ladder where you can go for a swim. Of course, there are people here as well but it does not feel as crowded as the beach. The water is deep here so it's for good swimmers only. Make sure you have snorkeling equipment or at least swim goggles with you. Some bread will also be useful, to feed the fish. The area is full of colourful fish, I felt like swimming in an aquarium. Last time I had an amazing experience like this was in Thailand…

Among the many luxurious and impressive villas, these two below are probably the most famous ones. I am sure you have seen them somewhere before, in a travel magazine or on the internet. I wonder who owns them… (As far as I know, Silvio Berlusconi, Giorgio Armani and Dolce & Gabbana all have a posh villa here.) Well, whoever owns them, I am jealous… Not so much for the villas—a small house would do it for me—but for the breathtaking location and for the balconies from where they can dive directly to the crystal clear Ligurian Sea.

Once you get to Portofino, you will realise that it is quite small and easy to discover. Life is mainly around the little bay with the fishing boats and the million-dollar yachts surrounded by the world-famous row of colourful houses. There are several fancy shops (Dior, Gucci, etc.) and restaurants around; if you are on a budget, it's better to avoid them. But you can still have a gelato on the piazza. If you enjoy reading gossip magazines about the life of famous people, keep your eyes open as you might run into the Beckhams, Jennifer Lopez or other VIPs here. Portofino used to be a tiny fishing village but it turned into a celebrity hotspot. It became the favourite destination of the rich and famous in the 1950s and 1960s when stars like Elizabeth Taylor, Brigitte Bardot and Ingrid Bergman spent their holidays here.

Wherever there are stars around, there will be paparazzi as well. The last time we were walking towards Portofino, we saw a man sitting by the sea holding a camera with a huge lens. He was watching the water and smoking, smiled at us and even greeted us when we passed him. First we thought he was a nature photographer, taking pictures of seagulls let's say. Then we soon realised that he was a paparazzo and he was interested in the luxury yachts out there, not the birds. Some days later, we saw a magazine at a petrol station; on its cover a couple was sunbathing naked on a nice boat. We did not know them but they must have been some very important celebrities.

Portofino really is stunning but it is also very crowded, I personally can't spend too much time there. To avoid the herds of tourists, climb up to the San Giorgio church; you will enjoy a wonderful view from the little piazza. If you want even less people and even better views, walk all the way up to the Brown Castle (Castello Brown). The castle is surrounded by a lush Italian garden and when you look at the panorama from its terrace, you will understand why Portofino has become so popular and famous. The entrance fee to the castle is 5 EUR. For some quiet time, visit the lighthouse (il Faro di Portofino) at the end of the promontory. From here, you can see the Ligurian coastline all the way to Tuscany.

Once you had enough of Portofino, catch the next boat or hike to San Fruttuoso.

San Fruttuoso

If you are following my recommended itinerary, you'll be arriving to San Fruttuoso from Portofino. You can take the boat from there or you can hike through the hills. Of course, if you prefer, you can also arrive from the other direction, from Camogli, either by boat or hiking. It is not accessible by car or train.

The hamlet of San Fruttuoso has a stunning location, in a hidden bay of the Portofino promontory, surrounded by the hills and forests of the Portofino Regional Park, far away from everything. The Abbey of San Fruttuoso of Capodimonte was built by Benedictine monks in the 10th century. Later, it was owned by the Doria family, the tombs of some family members can be found in the crypt. The Doria also built the square watch tower in the 16th century to defend San Fruttuoso.

Today, the abbey is the property of a national conservation fund (FAI). The nice stone building is standing right on the beach. However, for centuries there was no beach here so the boats were moored right under the arcades. Today, you will also see some fishing boats there. There is a tiny fishing village near the abbey, some trattorias and two beautiful beaches with crystal blue waters. If you would like to visit the abbey and the tower, there is an entrance ticket of a few euros.

Opening times change throughout the year, so please check at the local tourist offices when you are in the region.

There is another interesting sight at San Fruttuoso, just off the coast. It's the Christ of the Abyss (Il Cristo degli Abissi), an underwater bronze statue of Jesus Christ. The 2.5-meter tall statue was put in the sea on August 22, 1954 and is still standing there, about 15 meters deep. It's a popular site for divers. The dive is fairly easy but if you don't dive, you can try snorkeling or you can take a boat out there on a calm day and look at the statue through the water. A replica of the statue can be seen in the church of San Fruttuoso..

To finish your circle around the Portofino peninsula, take the boat or hike to Camogli. If you would like to hike this section, I recommend that you get a hiking map in one of the tourist offices in the area. There are more trails between San Fruttuoso and Camogli. The coastal path towards the Batterie is only recommended to expert hikers as there are some difficult and scary sections where you have to hold on to chains. You should avoid this part if you suffer from vertigo but go for it if you love adrenalin.

Camogli

Camogli was one of the nicest surprises for me in Liguria, it's just gorgeous! While nearby Portofino and Cinque Terre are world-famous tourist destinations, Camogli is still a well-kept secret. This slow-paced little town is, however, quite popular with North-Italians. During the past few years, it has become one of my favourite places in Liguria. In my next life, I would love to be a retired man in Camogli.

The picturesque beach of Camogli is lined by a row of tall houses, so-called palazzi. Some of them even have 8 floors. The houses are painted in different shades of pink, yellow, orange, green and terracotta, with green or yellow shutters. Around the windows, you can see trompe l'oeil paintings typical in Liguria. Camogli has always been a fishing village and these tall, colourful houses helped the fishermen find their way home when they were far out on the sea.

Under the houses there is a nice seaside promenade with wonderful bars, cafes and focaccia shops. It's one of those places where you could just sit around for hours with an aperol spritz or two and watch the waves or the sunset behind the church. If you walk around the church, you will find the fishing harbour of Camogli with restaurants, art shops and a lighthouse at the end of the pier. I love taking photos of the drying fishing nets with the colourful houses in the background.

If you walk one block up from the beach, you will find the main street of Camogli with regular shops and the railway station. If you were following my advice and arrived here having visited Santa Margherita Ligure, Portofino and San Fruttuoso, this is where you will finish your day. Maybe watch the sunset here then take an evening train back to the village where you are staying. Of course, you can do the whole circle the other way around but I think the lights are much better this way which is an important issue if you take lots of photos like me. You could also spend the entire day in Camogli, enjoy the laid back atmosphere and relax on the beach.

If you are in the area around the second Sunday of May, watch out for the Camogli Fish Festival and visit it if you can.

Beyond the Riviera di Levante

Riviera di Ponente

For about ten years, I've been travelling around the Riviera di Levante and the Cinque Terre. I have discovered basically every village and town along the coast, all the way from Tuscany to Genova. I was always wondering, what's on the other side of Genova, in the western part of Liguria. So I have started to visit this area as well, the Riviera di Ponente, which starts around Genova and goes all the way to the French border.

As I am really passionate about the Riviera di Levante, I was curious to see the other side. Am I going to like it? Or is it going to disappoint me? Well, I have to admit that it is much nicer than I expected. It is true that the coast is more built up so it is not so wildly beautiful, there are many bigger towns, some of them without much character, and you also find some industrial zones along the way, but there are many hidden gems around. You just have to know where to go. Also, there are long sandy beaches perfect for families, many resort towns with all the comforts and services, as well as more nightlife.

Train connections are not as good as in the Riviera di Levante, but there are local buses everywhere. Probably the best solution is to have a car, but parking is very difficult along the beaches in the main season. Don't forget that this area is very popular among Italian families, mainly from nearby Piemonte, but you will also meet thousands of tourists coming from Germany, Switzerland and France.

If you want to get to your destination quickly, use the A10 Autostrada, which is also called Fiori Autostrada. I love this drive as on one side you can see the beautiful Ligurian hills while on the other side you have seaview. You'll be driving through numerous tunnels and over very high bridges built over the valleys. However, if you have more time and the traffic is not so bad, drive on the road right by the sea, the so called Via Aurelia, it will take you through the charming coastal towns. (Not recommended in August.) This wonderful coastal drive also saves you money as this road is free while the autostrada is very expensive, like everywhere else in Italy.

The Riviera di Ponente is geographically divided into two parts: the Riviera delle Palme (Riviera of the Palms) between Genova and Capo Mele, and the Riviera dei Fiori (Riviera of the Flowers) between the French border and Capo Mele. These names already refer to the lush Mediterranean vegetation of the area. You'll find seaside promenades aligned with palm trees all over the place, while the Riviera of the Flowers is famous for its flower-growing industry. We also stopped to buy some unique agave and cacti into our own garden.

We have visited both areas, and would have loved to cross over to France as well, but unfortunately did not have time. There was too much to see on the Italian side. Below you can read about some of my favourite places in this part of Liguria. They are definitely worth a visit.

Varigotti

Varigotti is the pearl of Western Liguria. It's kind of like Portofino on the other side, very popular among VIPs as well. First I was hoping to stay there, but accommodation seemed too expensive, especially in the high season. It would have been very comfortable as we ended up on Varigotti's beach quite often in the crazy heat of July, it has become our favourite place for swimming and sunbathing. This beach was just amazing. The water was crystal clear and really warm, our baby girl loved it as well. We celebrated her first birthday here, and she swam in the sea for the first time in her life. Pretty good birthday present I guess. Needless to say, she loved it and so did we!

You can't miss Varigotti if you are travelling in this area. Look for the old part of the village with the orange, yellow and pink Saracen houses, tiny allies and characteristic piazzas right on the beach. We really enjoyed swimming in front of these historical buildings. There is another very famous beach here, the Bay of the Saracens. You have to leave Varigotti village and start driving towards Noli. It's an amazing beach with white sand, very popular and as a result parking is basically impossible. So arrive early, or maybe it's better to walk or take the local bus.

Noli

Noli is another favourite if you are looking for a nice beach with sand and small pebbles. While father and daughter were playing in the turquoise sea, I really enjoyed walking around and taking photos of the colourful fishing boats and nets. Although we were there in July, the beach did not feel crowded at all. Noli has a pretty seaside promenade with many palm trees and bougainvilleas. Make sure you also walk around the medieval town center where you will find several bars and restaurants as well as cute little shops. Noli is listed among the most beautiful villages of Italy. If you are lucky, you'll also bump into the lively street market.

Finalborgo

You also find Finalborgo on the list of the most beautiful villages of Italy. It can be found just inland from Finale Ligure, a famous resort town. The village is surrounded by a medieval wall and once you enter on one of the gates, you will find yourself in a very welcoming and relaxing atmosphere, a perfectly preserved historical center. It's a great place to get away from the beach crowds during summer months and enjoy a nice lunch or gelato on one of the squares. Try the borage ravioli made with herbs of the area. You can also find some interesting craft shops in Finalborgo. The town is a well-known center for outdoor activities, mainly rock climbing and mountain biking.

Borgio Verezzi

Another one of Italy's most beautiful villages, situated between Finale Ligure and Pietra Ligure. You have to drive up a winding road to this small medieval village. From the village you can see a breathtaking view of the ligurian coastline and it is one of the best places to watch the sunset. Borgio Verezzi is hosting a famous theatre festival every summer, people were gathering for the evening play when we were there. It was a bit awkward, as everyone was quite elegant while we just arrived from the beach. I was a bit sad because we could not enjoy the small piazza and I could not take a nice photo of it as it was covered by the stage and the chairs. Plus we also missed the sunset. We'll just have to go back I guess.

Dolceacqua

You definitely have to leave the beach and spend some time inland as well. The Ligurian hills are full of charming towns and villages, such as Apricale, Castelvecchio, Triora, Zuccarello, Colletta di Castelbianco... They are usually 20-30 minutes away from the coast. Probably the most famous of them is Dolceacqua, a much photographed medieval town in the Val Nervia. The historical part of the town and the new area are connected by a pretty humpback stone bridge, while the

Doria Castle dominates the whole view. In the old part you will find many artisan shops and bars in the narrow alleys, where you should not miss the famous Rossese wine. Dolceacqua also inspired Monet, he made several paintings of the town. He really loved the bridge and wrote about it as a "jewel of lightness".

Hanbury Botanic Gardens

The Hanbury Botanic Gardens can be found between Ventimiglia and the French border on a small winding road. We actually drove by and missed it as the entrance gate was under scaffolding. Don't expect a big parking area or crowds, you can easily park on the side of the road and there won't be too many people around. The 18-hectare garden is situated between the panorama road at about 100 meters above sea level and the sea, so the area is quite steep. It was established by Sir Thomas Hanbury in the 19th century, at that time they counted close to 6,000 different species from all over the world. The gardens are now operated by the University of Genova and at the moment there are about 2,500 kinds of plants. I love Mediterranean-style gardening, so for us this was a must. But even if you are not a garden lover, you can easily spend hours walking around, sitting in the shade and enjoying the view of the Ligurian Sea. There is also a small bar and a picnic area at the bottom.

Because of the extreme heat and because of travelling with a baby we did not see half of the things we wanted to see. So we are surely returning to this area soon. We are planning to visit more charming villages among the hills. We drove through Cervo and it was so beautiful, but we did not have time to stop, so have to go back. Same with Ventimiglia, the houses of the old town looked stunning. In Ventimiglia there is also a colourful Friday market, and I really need a new leather bag... I'd also love to cross the border and check out Menton, it looks so pretty on the photos. And besides all of this, we would love to spend more time on the tranquil beaches of the Riviera di Ponente.

Tuscany

The Cinque Terre is only a few kilometers away from the Tuscan border, so many travellers visit Tuscany before or after the Cinque Terre. As I have travelled around Tuscany many times and know it very well, I can help you plan your itinerary and book a room or apartment in a wonderful farmhouse (agriturismo) for you. You can also rent an entire house for your family if you prefer.

Tuscany is one of Italy's most beautiful regions, with a great variety of landscapes and uncountable treasures. Rolling hills with cypresses, vineyards, silver olive groves, poppy fields, sunflowers, medieval villages, stone farmhouses, sandy beaches, small islands, rocky mountain peaks, ski hills, world famous Renaissance pieces of art, Michelangelo, Leonardo, Giotto, simple dishes of the countryside, delicious red wine, golden olive oil... Tuscany is all of this, and so much more. To get an idea of the Tuscan atmosphere.

I am sure if you are planning a visit to Tuscany, Firenze, Siena and Pisa are on your agenda. The Internet and guidebooks are full of information about them, so I am not writing about these towns on this page. (But I do show you some of my favourite photos of these towns below.) Instead, I would like to write about some of my favourite villages and areas in Tuscany, which I highly recommend visiting.

But first of all, an important thing: in order to get a real feel for Tuscany, you should drive! So if possible, come by car or rent a car, and drive around. Look at the map and choose the smallest roads possible to get the best views. You don't see much from the motorways. The roads are winding but good quality and there is usually not much traffic. I often stopped in the middle of the road to take photos. And believe me, you want to stop every minute to take another amazing shot. Nature is so beautiful here. Poppies in spring, sunflowers in summer, grapes, olives, cypresses, forests all around. And those rolling hills! I am in love.

Of course Tuscany would not be Tuscany without those adorable hilltop villages and the medieval farmhouses all over the place. Many of these houses can be rented for your holiday, send me an e-mail if you'd like me to recommend some nice ones for you.

As this just not is not about Tuscany, I am not going to write a novel here, even if I could. (Frances Mayes has done that before me.) I am just quickly going to mention some of my favourite places that are really worth a visit.

Chianti

When you are in Tuscany, you just can't miss the Chianti region. It is situated between Firenze and Siena, and is a very famous wine region. I could drive around the Chianti for weeks and never get bored. In a way, it's always the same: vineyards, olives and farmhouses, but the view is different after every curve. And always picture perfect. Then at the end of that small road, you'll come to a tiny village with a cute piazza, a church, a couple of houses, and if you are lucky, the weekly market. Don't forget to taste some Chianti wine. If you would like to book a wine or olive oil tasting, maybe visit an olive harvest, just send me an email and I'll help you organise it.

Montefioralle

I found Montefioralle by accident when I was driving around the Chianti. It's located very close to Greve in Chianti. It quickly became one of my favourite villages in Tuscany, and I have returned several times. Sometimes I was the only tourist in the village, I only met some local ladies sitting in front of their doors. There is a narrow street that runs around the village, it's very pleasant to walk along the old stone houses. Montefioralle is listed among the most beautiful villages of

Italy. (I borghi piú belli d'Italia.) You also find a very good restaurant here, Taverna del Guerrino, with an amazing view of the Chianti hills.

Volpaia

Another very pretty village in the Chianti hills. Look for the signs along the road between Greve and Rhadda in Chianti, you'll have to turn off onto a smaller road. Volpaia is surrounded by vineyards, olive groves and forests, and you can enjoy a fantastic panorama of the Chianti hills. Chianti Classico has been made here for centuries. Many houses are owned by the Castello di Volpaia winery, there is a system of wine cellars underneath. Don't miss a wine tasting here, and if you get hungry, head to the restaurant "La Bottega", which is quite famous in this area. In Volpaia I felt like walking around in medieval times.

Monteriggioni

You can see Monteriggioni from the Firenze–Siena autostrada, it's quite a sight. It's a very well preserved walled castle, dating back to the 13th century. The wall with the 14 towers is really impressive. Inside the wall there is a nice piazza and a couple of streets. It's really worth the stop. A famous medieval festival takes place here every July.

Lucca

Lucca is a wonderful town, one of my favourites. It's very close to Pisa, so you can easily visit the two places during a daytrip from your farmhouse or even from the Cinque Terre. The best way to discover the town is by bike, you'll find several rental shops. First ride around the 4km town wall, which surrounds the historical center. Then, during siesta time, when the streets are almost empty, you can easily bike all around Lucca, and visit the numerous pretty squares. For a great view, climb up Torre Guinigi. When you get hungry, you can choose from many wonderful restaurants. In the evening, you can listen to Puccini operas all year around.

Vinci

Everyone knows the name Vinci, but not many people know that Leonardo was actually born in Vinci, a small town in Tuscany. In Vinci everything is about the Renaissance genius, there is a Leonardo museum, but you can also see the house where he was born. Vinci is surrounded by beautiful countryside, I can imagine that it really inspired the master. I envy Leonardo not only because he was an incredibly talented Renaissance man, but also because he spent a part of his life in this picture-perfect place.

Garfagnana

When you think about Tuscany, you'll probably think about rolling hills, vineyards and cypresses, and not about high mountains and ski hills. But this is also Tuscany. In the northern part of Tuscany, in the Apuane Alps you can find an exciting mix of Tuscan and alpine atmosphere. It is a hiker's paradise with many hiking trails. The Garfagnana valley lies between these mountains and it's really worth the visit. If you are driving from Lucca, don't forget to stop at the medieval Devil's bridge. (Ponte del Diavolo). My favourite town around here is Barga, its typical Tuscan houses look great with the mountains in the background. During the winter several ski hills operate in this area.

Pitigliano

I had been travelling around Tuscany for years when I finally made it to the very south of Tuscany, the Maremma region. I totally fell in love with this area, it was breathtaking and so relaxing after the crowds in Firenze or Pisa. Hardly any tourists, empty streets and piazzas. When we first drove by Pitigliano I couldn't believe my eyes, it looked like a town from a fairy tale. It is standing on top of tufa rocks, above the Lente valley. You should get lost in the narrow streets and admire the huge wooden doors, fountains, old steps and pretty courtyards. Around the central piazza, you will find some restaurants and cafés. Pitigliano is also on the list of the most beautiful villages of Italy.

Sorano

Sorano is located not far from Pitigliano and the two towns are actually quite similar. Sorano is also standing on top of tufa rocks, and even the houses look like they had been carved out of these rocks. Another place without tourist invasion. Walking around Sorano felt like jumping back to medieval times, only some TV antennas made me realise that I was in the 21st century. Amazing place! I was shocked that my very good Tuscany guidebook didn't even mention Sorano.

Sovana

Pitigliano, Sorano and Sovana are all very close to each other, you can visit all three of them in a day. Sovana is also listed among the most beautiful villages of Italy and I can see why. Try the wine of Sovana, which was made already in Etruscan times. They also make one of the most delicious olive oils in Tuscany.

Saturnia

Well, if you have visited all the above villages and towns, you really deserve to relax. Go to Saturnia and find the famous outdoor waterfalls, the Cascate del Gorello and the Cascate del Mulino. These natural thermal springs have a temperature of around 37°C and are very relaxing. Sit under a small waterfall and you also get a nice back massage. The only downside is that it's awfully hard to get out

Acitivities

Outdoor

Hiking

The villages and sanctuaries of the Cinque Terre are connected by 100 km of trails. You can hike in amazing places through forests, vineyards, olive groves, mediterranean flowers and tiny villages. The views towards the bright green terraces and the deep blue sea are breathtaking. I think you can't really see and understand the Cinque Terre if you don't do any hiking. So don't just rush through the 5 villages by train or boat in a single day! Try to spend more days here and discover the Cinque Terre National Park on foot. Of course, you need a good fitness level to do that, as there are many ups and downs and long flights of steps in the area.

When hiking, take enough water with you! On the path, between two villages, there is usually no water available. In the villages, you can always find a fountain to refill your bottle and even in the smallest village or at the sanctuaries, you can find a bar.

Summer on the trails can be really hot as there is not much shade. You should start early, spend the early afternoon swimming or relaxing in the shade, and then continue hiking late afternoon. If you come to the Cinque Terre more for hiking than swimming, come in April, May, September or October for a more pleasant climate.

The path can be quite narrow and there is no railing, so mind your step! Some sections are not recommended if you suffer from vertigo. I have to admit that I do suffer from vertigo in some situations but I've never had any problems on any of the Cinque Terre trails. For hiking, I recommend hiking shoes or hiking sandals. Avoid flip flops!

In case of bad weather or maintenance work, some sections can be closed. You usually find a posted notice about this in the villages, or you can ask for information in the Information Centers of the National Park. You can also buy hiking maps there.

You can find the list and map of hiking trails on the website of the Cinque Terre National Park. Here you can see how long is a path, how much time it takes going there and coming back, depending on which way is up of course. The map also shows which path is closed. At the Information Center, they'll be happy to help you choose between the many trails, depending on your fitness level and the number of days you spend in the area. But let me also share my favourite hikes with you.

My favourite hikes

Corniglia Volastra Manarola
If you only have time for one hike, do this one! If you prefer joining a guide, try this hiking tour with wine tasting.

Riomaggiore Telegrafo Portovenere

It's a full day hike with marvellous views. From Portovenere, you can come back by boat or bus & train.

Sant'Antonio Campiglia Monesteroli
The Monesteroli steps and the whole Tramonti area are just unbelievable and off the beaten track. For more information, read the Tramonti page. There are many, I mean MANY steps going down to the village, and you also have to come back. Not a good option if you have problems with your knees.

Vernazza Monterosso

On the higher trail, passing the two sanctuaries, with the best views of Vernazza and some really wild sections.

Monterosso - Levanto

A wonderful, relaxed hike with the panorama of the entire Cinque Terre coastline and also the Bay of Levanto on the other side.

You are probably wondering why I don't mention the famous coastal path of the Cinque Terre, the Sentiero Azzurro (Blue path) which connects the 5 villages. Unfortunately this path was damaged by floods and landslides during the past years. The Via dell'Amore between Riomaggiore and Manarola is closed. (UPDATE: A very short section between Manarola and the bar has been opened.) The Manarola-Corniglia section is basically ready but we are still waiting for the National Park to open it. Corniglia-Vernazza is open. Vernazza-Monterosso is open. This might change, so for updated information ask at the National Park Centers. For the coastal path, you have to buy the Cinque Terre Card, even if only one section is open. All the other trails in the area are free, including my favourite ones mentioned above. UPDATE MARCH 2018: THE ENTIRE BLUE PATH IS CLOSED AT THE MOMENT!

Don't forget, that many path are waiting for you also outside the Cinque Terre National Park. Liguria is a hiker's paradise! You could walk for months and never get bored of the breathtaking views of the colourful villages, nature and the sea. You could basically walk all the way to France on the beautiful Ligurian trails.

Biking

People often ask me this question: "Should we take our bikes to the Cinque Terre?" Well, my short answer is "no". My longer answer is "maybe, it depends". If you are staying in Riomaggiore, Manarola, Corniglia or Vernazza, don't take it. These villages are full of steep streets and stairs, not ideal for bikes. If you have to bring your bicycle with you, by all means, because let's say you are travelling to Tuscany or Lake Garda afterwards, make sure you book an accommodation which is not at the top of those 100 steps, and check with your accommodation provider if you could store the bikes in the room or apartment. I can help you find a place to stay where it is not a problem, just send me an e-mail. If you are staying in Monterosso or Levanto, the situation is better, as those villages are more flat and local people cycle around as well.

The area is mainly for hiking but if you are in excellent shape and don't mind really steep and long climbs with your bike, you could basically cycle on the car road above the Cinque Terre villages. There are also some good trails for mountain biking, ask for information at the local offices of the National Park. If you'd rather go with a local guide, I recommend this mountain bike tour. Your guide will also provide mountain bikes if you don't have your own. An easier option is the EBike tour, where you will bike above Levanto, Bonassola and Framura.

There is one activity I recommend to everyone, regardless of age or fitness level: ride on the bicycle path from Levanto to Framura. (See the photo at the top of this page, and also the one below.) It's scenic, flat, easy and fun! It's about 5.5 km long and takes about 30 minutes if you don't stop anywhere. Take the train to Levanto and rent a bike there. I like Fabio's "Sensafreni Bike Shop" on Piazza del Popolo. Their phone number is +39 0187 807128. It's better to book your bikes ahead, especially in the main season. If you are on your honeymoon, I recommend their tandem bikes. These are their rental prices for 2015 for city bikes:

- ✓ 1 hour - 3 EUR.
- ✓ 3.5 hours (9:00AM-12:30PM, 12:30PM-4:00PM or 4:00PM-7:30PM) - 5 EUR.
- ✓ 7 hours (9:00AM-4:00PM) - 8 EUR.
- ✓ 10.5 hours (9:00AM-7:30PM) - 10 EUR.
- ✓ 24 hours - 15 EUR.
- ✓ Child seat - 2 EUR for the entire rental time.
- ✓ There are child bikes available in about 10 different sizes, prices are the same.

✓ Tandem bikes: 1 hour - 5 EUR, 9:00AM-7:30PM - 20 EUR.

Once you have your bike and get to the beach, turn right, and at the end of Levanto you will find the start of the path. This bike road was opened in 2010, following the old, 19th-century railway tracks. It's a wonderful experience, the path goes all along the sea, through many tunnels. Kids will love it as well! You can also go running or walking there. Along the path, you will find some tiny bays, perfect for a swim. I love these beaches as they can only be reached by boat or bike, so they are not so crowded. The path is really good quality. You need lights for the tunnels and also take a pullover as it can be cool in there even on hot summer days. It's a great half-day trip but you can also make it a full-day excursion: visit Levanto, bike to Bonassola, visit Bonassola, go for a swim and have lunch there, bike to Framura, visit Framura and have a drink there, then ride back to Levanto. There are plans to make this path longer, all the way from Monterosso to Deiva Marina. I can't wait!

Swimming and beaches

Travelers often rush through the Cinque Terre in a day or two and don't spend a longer summer holiday here, as they think there are no good beaches in this area. Well, it's true that the Cinque Terre is not famous for its long sandy beaches, but for me, the sea around here is so much more exciting. The coastline is varied, full of small bays and beaches, some of them in the middle of nature, others just below the colourful houses of a fishing village. The wonderfully turquoise Ligurian Sea is all around you, so you can enjoy sightseeing, hiking or eating, then jump in the water wherever you feel like it. If you prefer more ordinary but still breathtaking beaches, you will find many close to the Cinque Terre so you can enjoy them doing short day trips. Once you see the photos below, I am pretty sure you will bring your swimsuit with you.

Riomaggiore has a beach with big rocks and pebbles. You can find it if you follow the path to the left from the little fishing harbour. It's in a beautiful natural environment, just rocks and sea. Don't look for locker rooms, showers or ice cream vendors here. Can be a bit difficult to walk around the big rocks but it's a nice place for a swim if you are staying in Riomaggiore.

Corniglia can be found 100 meters above sea level so many believe that the village does not have a beach. Well, there are actually 3 areas for swimming around here. My favourite is the hidden little bay behind and below the village. You can reach it following the Marina sign. Of course, you have to walk down many steps, for about 5 minutes. To me, this is paradise! The water is beautiful and clean, and while you are swimming, you can enjoy the view of the green terraces in the background. The water is deep, so for good swimmers only.

You can find a beach below the railway station of Corniglia. You have to go down the steps at the station and start walking towards Manarola. When you get to the end of the row of old cabins on your left, you will find an entrance to an underpass. It's kind of hard to notice first, so look for it! The steps will take you down to the beach. You will also see some directions written on the ground. Alternatively, you can keep going and you will find some steps on your right going down to the beach. The last time I was there, the bottom part of the steps was missing but it was replaced by a wooden ladder. So it's a bit of an adventure to get there but you will find a nice relaxed beach with big stones, many of them are beautifully shaped by the elements of nature.

If you are even more adventurous, visit the secluded Guvano beach between Corniglia and Vernazza. You can reach it through an old railway tunnel. Walk down the Lardarina steps from Corniglia, turn right and walk towards the lonely house there. You will find the tunnel entrance near the house. I am not sure what the current situation is but the last time I was there, it was open. The tunnel is completely dark, so take a good flashlight with you. You'll be walking in pitch dark for about 20 minutes and at some points you will feel that it's just an endless tunnel. Someone even called it a "horror tunnel". But don't worry, it will end and you will find yourself on the other side of Corniglia, in a beautiful oasis of olive trees. From here, you can descend to the beach on a steep path. If you are scared in the dark or feel claustrophobic but still would love to see this beach, just rent a boat and get to Guvano from Vernazza.

It's a "clothing optional" beach so only go there if nude people do not bother you. There are usually not too many people around so you can surely find a peaceful corner for your towel. If you are looking for a secret, wild beach, totally immersed in nature, don't miss Guvano. One warning though: I was told that sometimes there are weird people around. So don't go alone as a woman, and don't take valuables with you. Otherwise, don't worry, just enjoy this magical place!

In Vernazza, there is a small sandy beach (good for kids as well), and you can also swim at the end of the pier, among the boats. (The water is deep here, so this area is for good swimmers only.) This is one of my favourite places; it is a fantastic experience to swim among the colourful boats with Vernazza's beautiful main square in the background.

During the horrible flood of October 25, 2011 Vernazza was devastated. At the same time, the forces of nature have created a new rocky beach. You can reach it from the main street, crossing a small tunnel.

In Monterosso, there are two long beaches with sand and pebbles. Most of the area is private with sun beds and beach umbrellas so you have to pay for it. However, there are also free beaches, for example in front of the railway station, or at the right end of the beach, towards the statue of the Giant. In front of the station, you can also use the locker rooms for a couple of euros. In the low season the entire beach is free.

For the best swimming experience along the Cinque Terre coastline, just rent a boat or book a boat tour from Manarola. When we went on the "Cinque Terre from the sea" tour we swam under a small waterfall, in a cave and stopped at a hidden beach, which was the smallest beach I have ever seen. It was a fantastic experience, the water had amazing colours and there was nobody around us. If you love swimming, you should not miss this experience.

If you are looking for traditional beaches with sand and pebbles, you can find many of them between the Cinque Terre and Genoa. They are all suitable for the whole family. Just hop on the train and go to Levanto. If you rent a bike and ride along the coastal bike path, you can enjoy the beaches of Levanto, Bonassola and Framura in the same day. Deiva Marina, Moneglia and Sestri Levante all have nice beaches perfect for kids.

If you do a day trip to Portofino, you can swim in many bays between Santa Margherita Ligure and Portofino. Also, 3 of my favourite swimming spots are around there. Paraggi is an absolute highlight, the water looks like in an exotic sea. This protected marine area is full of fish so take your snorkeling equipment and some bread with you. San Fruttuoso is another must, with its 10th-century abbey right at the beach. To finish a wonderful trip around the Portofino peninsula, go for a swim in Camogli and watch the colourful palazzi glowing in the lights of the setting sun.

Another day, discover the Gulf of Poets. Go to Portovenere, you will also find some beaches along the way. You can take the ferry or water taxi to Palmaria island and swim there. On the other side of the gulf, marvellous sandy beaches are waiting for you around Lerici and Tellaro.

Water sports

The marine area around the Cinque Terre has been a national park since 1997. We can find interesting rock formations, flora and fauna under the water as well. As I don't dive, I don't have any personal experience but I do recommend the diving center of Riomaggiore. Their shop can be found in the tunnel leading to the little fishing harbour of Riomaggiore. There are also a couple of diving centers in Levanto. They can be found on the beach, at the right end if you are facing the sea. For divers, I highly recommend a visit to San Fruttuoso and the Christ of the Abyss. Underwater life in the entire Portofino area is amazing. You can find several diving centers in Santa Margherita Ligure.

If you don't dive, you should at least try snorkeling. Make sure you have your snorkeling equipment or at least swim goggles with you. If you don't have any of these, you can rent them in the diving centers. I've seen plenty of fish off the beach of Riomaggiore and in the bay of Manarola, but my top snorkeling experience was in Paraggi.

If you prefer to be above water, why not try sailing, a boat tour from Manarola, a kayak tour along the coastline, fishing from Monterosso or fishing from Vernazza? I can also help you to rent boats or canoes, just send me an e-mail.

On windy days, Levanto is a very popular surf beach. You can find a surf school here and you can rent surf boards as well.

Culture

Churches and oratories

Riomaggiore

Church of San Giovanni Battista
The church was built in 1340 but in 1870 the facade was rebuilt in a Neo-Gothic style. The Gothic doors on the right side, the rose window, the wooden crucifix and the organ from 1851 are all well worth seeing. From the square in front of the church, you can enjoy a wonderful

view of the village. I love walking up here at night, Riomaggiore is really pretty with the lights.

Oratory of San Rocco
The oratory can be found next to the castle. It was built in the 15th century in remembrance of the plague in the village.

Manarola

Church of San Lorenzo
The church, which was built in 1338, has a Gothic facade with a nice rose window, and a Baroque-style interior. On the facade, there is a bas-relief representing the martyrdom of San Lorenzo. On the 15th-century triptych, you can see San Lorenzo with other saints. The church can be found in the upper part of the village. On the same square, you will find a 14th-century oratory and a bell tower from the 13th century, originally built as a watch tower.

Corniglia

Church of San Pietro: The 14th-century church is one of the most interesting monuments of the Ligurian Gothic style. The rose window on the facade is made of white Carrara marble, and it has Corniglia's ancient symbol, a deer, in the middle. Make sure you walk inside as well, you will see a 12th-century christening font and a polyptych.

Oratory of the Disciplinati of Santa Caterina

The 18th-century monument stands above the Largo Taragio square. You can enjoy a beautiful view from behind the oratory.

Vernazza

Church of Santa Margarita d'Antiochia: The church, which stands on the main square of Vernazza, was constructed in 1318 in Ligurian Gothic style. Its belltower is 40 meters high and has an octogonal shape. At an open-air art festival, there was a rope connecting the belltower with a temporary tower on the other side of the beach. As part of the show, the belltower went up in flames and a rope dancer escaped, walking on the rope high above the little harbour. It was an amazing experience!

Monterosso

Convent of Cappuccini and Church of San Francesco: The convent with the church can be found on top of the San Cristoforo hill. It was built in 1619 and, during the centuries, it was used as hospital and warehouse as well until it was returned to its rightful owners. Among other artwork, you can also see Van Dyck's Crucifixion inside. Next to the church, you will find the cemetery.

Church of San Giovanni Battista: The 13th-century church is located in the historical center of Monterosso, and is another nice example of Ligurian Gothic style. Its beautiful facade is comprised of alternating strips of white marble and green serpentine. Its belltower was originally part of Monterosso's defence system, used as a watch tower. The Baroque altar dates back to 1744.

Oratory of Confraternita dei Neri: The 16th-century Baroque oratory can be found in the old town of Monterosso, near the church of San Giovanni Battista.

Oratory of Confraternita dei Bianchi, Santa Croce: This oratory is located in the old town of Monterosso as well, behind the church of San Giovanni Battista. So within a few steps, you can see three interesting sights. You should spend some time inside the oratory as well, the 19th-century organ is well worth seeing.

Portovenere

Church of San Pietro: This church was constructed in 1277 over the ruins of another church dedicated to Venus. Venus is *Venere* in Italian, while *Porto* means harbour, so that's where the name of the town comes from. The Genoan-Gothic building is beautiful with its black and white stripes, perched on top of a rock in the sea. Next to the church, don't miss the Romanesque style arcades with amazing view towards the Cinque Terre.

Church of San Lorenzo: The Romanesque style church was built in the 12th century. Unfortunately, it was badly damaged during the centuries and had to be rebuilt several times.

Levanto

Church of Sant Andrea: The 13th-century church is a nice example of Ligurian Gothic style. Its facade is comprised of alternating white and dark green strips with a white marble rose window.

Castles and towers

Riomaggiore

Castle: Not much is known about the castle that stands on top of the hill between the Rio Maggiore and the Rio Finale river valleys. According to historians, it was built in the second part of the 13th century for defence purposes. In case of attacks from the sea, the inhabitants were hiding here. During the 19th century, it was used as a cemetery. Today, it is a center for conferences, cultural events and weddings. The castle can be easily found if you follow the signs. Although you have to climb a few steps, the wonderful view is definitely worthwhile.

Manarola

Bastion: Manarola's castle was probably built in the 13th century. Unfortunately, today, you can only see the remains of the bastion, surrounded by colourful houses.

Vernazza

Doria castle and Belforte tower: The round tower of the castle of this Genoan noble family is still an important building in Vernazza. From the Belforte tower, you can enjoy a magnificent view of the village and its colourful harbour. There is another tower higher up, along the walking path leading to Corniglia.

Monterosso

Aurora tower: The 16th-century Aurora tower is located by the sea, at the foot of the hill of the Cappuccini. This tower is fortunately in good condition.

Portovenere

Andrea Doria castle: The castle, which took the Genoan centuries (from the 12th to the 17th) to build, dominates the town of Portovenere. Several towers of the local defence system are still in good condition. From the castle, you can enjoy a fantastic view over the St. Peter church and the sea.

Levanto

Castle and Clock Tower: If you start walking up the hill towards Monterosso, you will find a nice historical area. The castle was built by the Malaspina family in the 11th century then later rebuilt by the Genoan people. For a long time, it served as a prison, today it is a private residence. The Clock Tower dates back to 1265. You can also see the remains of the medieval city walls.

Festivals, national holidays

Italians love to party so they always find a reason. They celebrate anchovies, eggplant, tomatoes, lemon, all the saints, pirates...

So almost every month there is a *FESTA* (festival) where the people of the village get together to eat, drink, dance, chat and watch the fireworks. In case of a religious holiday, the mass and the procession are also important parts of the *FESTA*.

In the Cinque Terre as well, from spring until fall, there are several fantastic festivals. Try to time your holiday so that you can attend one of these local events.

January

Manarola nativity scene
Manarola is worth a visit during winter as well, as for the holiday season, Mario Andreoli turns the hillside of Manarola into a huge nativity scene. The 300 characters are made of recycled materials and are placed in a different way every year. Of course, the nativity scene is the most beautiful at night, illuminated. You can see it from the start of December until the end of January. Different scenes are illuminated on August 10, the day of San Lorenzo, and at Easter time which you can see on the photo. It's possible to rent rooms with great views of the nativity scene.

January 6 La Befana
In the Italian folklore, Befana is an old woman with a big nose. She wears an old coat and a black shawl, and her big bag is full of gifts and

candies. She flies around on a broomstick and on January 6, she visits all the children of Italy. She enters the houses through the chimney and puts the gifts in old socks. Traditionally, only good kids get presents, while bad kids receive coal. Today coal is usually replaced by dark candy and there is usually a few pieces in each sock.

April

Italy's liberation the end of World War II in Italy is celebrated on this special day.

May

May 1 Labour day
Italians also celebrate this day with processions in the streets.

Monterosso Sagra dei limoni
The Monterosso Lemon festival is held on a weekend in May. Local people participate in different competitions. You can see who grew the biggest lemon in his garden and who can make the nicest statue out of lemon. Of course, several lemon delicacies can be tasted. Don't miss the limoncino and the lemon pie!

June

June 2 Republic day
On June 2, 1946, a constitutional referendum was held. The people of Italy voted to end the monarchy and Italy became a republic. (They did not like the monarchy as the king supported Mussolini.) The last king, Umberto II and his family escaped from the country.

Monterosso Corpus Christi

On the second Sunday after Pentecost, the streets of Monterosso are decorated with thousands of flowers and petals. In the evening, a procession crosses the historical center.

In Italy, all towns and villages have a patron saint. The saint's day is usually celebrated with procession, music, dancing, eating, drinking and fireworks.

June 24 Riomaggiore The day of San Giovanni Battista
June 24 is also Midsummer Day.

June 24 Monterosso The day of San Giovanni Battista
In Monterosso, people celebrate with delicious anchovy dishes and a fantastic firework at night.
June 29 Corniglia The day of San Pietro and Paolo
A large traditional cake, the "Torta dei Fieschi" is made on this special day. A taste is offered to all the participants of the festival on the main square of Corniglia.

July

July 20 Vernazza The day of Santa Margarita
In Vernazza, the patron saint is celebrated with an evening procession which starts from the main square and finishes at the end of the village.

July 24-25 Levanto Festa del Mare The day of San Giacomo and the celebration of the sea
The highlight of the two-day festival is when large crosses are carried along the main street of Levanto. At the start of the procession, you

can see the statue of the saint. The 100 kg crosses are being carried by very strong local men, taking turns. It is a honour to carry the cross, all local men want to do it at least once in their life. When everyone gets down to the sea, thousands of candles are let to float on the water which is an amazing sight. The day is finished with fireworks which you can enjoy from the deck chairs on the beach

August

August 10 Manarola The day of San Lorenzo
On the day of San Lorenzo, you can watch the procession in Manarola and how the sea is blessed. On this day, several artists arrive to paint in the villages and on the hiking trails. According to the legend, during this night, you have to watch the summer sky and if you see a falling star, you have to make a wish. The falling stars are believed to be the teardrops of San Lorenzo.

August 15 Ferragosto
This seems to be the most important Italian holiday. It was known already in Roman times, originally related to the end of hard summer works in the fields. The Catholic Church celebrates August 15 as the day of Assumption of the Virgin Mary. That's when Italians usually start their summer vacation which lasts until the start of the school year, around the middle of September.

August 17 Portovenere Festa della Madonna Bianca

If you can, come to Portovenere on August 17th. It is the day of the Festa della Madonna Bianca, my favourite festival in the area. In the evening, the rocks and the Church of San Pietro are illuminated by hundreds of huge candles, it is an absolutely breathtaking sight!

August Vernazza Festa dei Pirati
At the Festival of the Pirates locals celebrate that many centuries ago Vernazza fought back the attacks of the Saracens. The festival does not have a certain date but it surely takes place during the summer.

September

Harvest
On the terraces of the Cinque Terre, harvest starts around the middle of September but of course it all depends on the weather.

Monterosso Anchovy and olive festival
This gastronomic festival is held every year in September. Here you can taste several local dishes made with the wonderful Monterosso anchovies.

November

Olive harvest
November is the month of olive picking. Colourful nets are spread under the trees and the olives are picked by hand while the higher branches are shaken by a machine. The olives are taken to the olive mill and soon you can taste the fresh, golden extra virgin. Read more about the olive harvest.

December

The above mentioned Manarola nativity scene can be seen from December 8.

Gastronomy

Wine

You cannot leave the Cinque Terre without tasting the local wine. Wine making has been a crucial part of the history of the Cinque Terre and the vineyards on the cultivated terraces make this stretch of coastline so unique. People have been making wine here for about a 1,000 years and as you cannot use machines on the terraces, work is done by hand even today. Since the 1970s however, there has been a significant improvement both in quality and quantity due to technical developments. A monorail system has been built to transport grapes, tools and people up and down the steep hills. The 50 small trains make the work and the harvest in the vineyards much easier and more efficient.

Both the white wine Cinque Terre DOC and the sweet dessert wine, the Sciacchetrá Cinque Terre DOC, are worth trying. On the label of Cinque Terre wines, you can see "DOC" (Denominazione di Origine Controllata) since 1973. This means quality wine with controlled origin and strict regulations.

Cinque Terre white wine is made with three different grapes: Bosco, Albarola and Vermentino. It goes well together with local dishes like seafood risotto, fried anchovies or pasta with pesto.

Sciacchetrá is made with the same three grapes. This delicious passito is made with the selection of the best grapes which are dried for about 2 months. It is usually consumed as dessert with typical Italian biscuits (biscotti, pandolce, panforte) dipped into the wine. It is an expensive wine so people usually keep a bottle for special occasions like weddings. When a child is born, it's nice to get a bottle of Sciacchetrá and only open it on the child's 18th birthday.

If you would like to taste local wines with an expert, check out these wine tasting programs. You can even meet the winegrower, visit his vineyard and wine cellar if you book the wine tour above Riomaggiore or the hike with wine tasting.

If you would like to read more about wine in the Cinque Terre, I recommend the beautiful book of Catherina Unger, Vineyards with seaview. (Vigneti con vista mare). I love reading her words about the passion of local people for their land. She introduces all the winegrowers of the Cinque Terre, talking about their history, present and future plans as well. Catherina is a passionate photographer, her beautiful photos accompany the texts. The book also makes a perfect gift for someone interested in wine.

Lemon and Limoncino

I have always loved lemon. It is not only delicious but healthy, fragrant and nice-looking as well. I like it in any form: ice cream, lemonade, cake or tea. In the villages of the Cinque Terre, I have taken several photos of lemons in colourful baskets or locally made ceramic bowls. The yellow of lemon and the blue of the Ligurian sea match so nicely...

Lemon trees are all over the place, almost everyone has one in the garden. There is even a lemon festival in Monterosso

Italian lemon and Limoncello are famous not only around Sorrento and in Sicily but in the Cinque Terre as well, thanks to the sunny climate. The tasty liqueur is called Limoncino here.

Local restaurants often offer you Limoncino at the end of the meal. If you visit a family, they will probably serve you their homemade liqueur. If you would like to take home this real mediterranean drink, you can buy it in any shop in the Cinque Terre. Of course, you can also make your own Limoncino.

Recipe for limoncino

- ✓ 5 big lemons
- ✓ 1 L 90% pure alcohol
- ✓ 1-1.5 L water
- ✓ 800 g sugar

Peel the lemon. Mix the yellow of the lemon zest with alcohol in a closed container and leave it to ferment for 4-5 days.

Dissolve sugar in water. Add less water if you would like a stronger liqueur. Add the water/sugar mixture to the container with lemon and let it ferment for another 5 days. At the end, filter well, fill it in bottles and put it into the freezer. Serve it in chilled glasses!

Olive

I've been planning for years a visit to the Cinque Terre villages during the olive harvest. Last year, I missed it by a few days so this year I was planning more seriously. I was constantly communicating with our host, Cesare, and the date changed at least four times. It happened not because of Italian mentality but because of the weather. In the end, we travelled between November 1 and 7, and before getting to Manarola, we even visited an olive harvest in Tuscany, in the Chianti region.

In Tuscany we stayed in a beautifully restored farmhouse which I highly recommend to anyone travelling to the Chianti. (I can help you with the booking.) In the 16th century, the farm belonged to the nephew of Michelangelo so Michelangelo used to get wine for the Pope from here.

Our timing was perfect. A long, rainy period just ended so we had pleasant, sunny weather most of the time. We saw colourful nets and people picking the olives all over the place while olive presses were working day and night both in Tuscany and Liguria. Once we got back home, huge rainfalls hit the area and we were shocked to see the floods on television. So again, the weather gods were taking care of me, just like every time I am in the Cinque Terre...

We had a team of three and we travelled to learn as much as possible about olives, take photos, make a short film and of course taste as many different olive oils as possible. We were three girls: Eszter is a journalist and makes videos, Alexa is a fantastic cook and writes a gastronomic blog at axi's kitchen while I am the Cinque Terre and Tuscany expert so I organise everything, take many photos and write on this site.

We are passionate about Italy, Italian food and wine. Our enthusiasm and good humour had no limits so everywhere we went people were happy to greet us and talk with the "journalist girls". By the end of the 7th day, we became experts of olive oil, of course only "amateur"-level experts. Our hosts Gabriele, Valentina, Andrea, Cesare and Alessandro are all fantastic people, they made great efforts to help us.

A few interesting facts about olive oil

According to historians, olive oil was made already around 5,000 B.C., first in ancient Greece, then in areas that are Israel and Egypt today. The olive tree arrived to the Apennine peninsula around 3000 B.C. This plant always had a great importance. It was the symbol of peace and well-being. Homer called olive oil liquid gold; at the ancient olympic games, the winner got an olive branch. And in the Bible, the pigeon that returns to Noah's ark was also carrying an olive branch.

Today, Italy is one of the biggest olive oil producers of the world. You can find olive trees in almost every Italian region except the north where the climate is not warm enough. There are hundreds of olive types, and the colour and the taste of olive oil is different in every region. Tuscan oil is green, peppery, spicy, a bit hot. Southern oils from Puglia, Sicily and Calabria are deep green with an intensive taste of fruits and almond. Ligurian oil has a light, golden yellow colour and a mild, fruity taste.

The colour, taste and quality of the oil depend on several factors: the type of olive, elevation, climate, soil, time of harvest, method of harvest and how quickly the olives get to the press. In the Chianti area, the high number of sunny hours and the big difference between day and night temperatures make the oil more spicy. In Liguria, the climate not too hot in the summer and not too cold in the winter creates a milder taste.

Cesare's olive grove can be found in Volastra, above Manarola. The view is just stunning: silver colour olive trees, green and orange nets for the picking, yellow vineyards and the deep blue Ligurian Sea in the background. While locals were working hard picking olives, we just couldn't stop taking photos.

In Liguria, there are no big quantities of olive oil as it is one of the smallest Italian regions, plus it is hard to grow anything on the steep slopes. Olive groves usually belong to families and they do the harvest between the start of November and end of January. Family and friends get together and finish picking within a few days.

So how do they harvest the olives?

First they spread the colourful nets under the trees so the fruit will fall on them. You can actually see these nets all year, wrapped up on the trees. The olive is picked mainly by hand and with a small instrument that looks like a toy rake. They sometimes hit the upper branches with a stick or use a small machine with a propeller-like end to hit the fruit off the tree. Cesare told us that they don't use the harvest machines that are often used on flat areas to shake the trees. The terraces of the Cinque Terre are too small for these machines but Cesare also thinks that these machines would hurt the tree. The trees here are young (20-30 years) and small so it is easy to reach even the upper branches. In Puglia where 40% of Italian olive oil is produced you can find really old trees with huge trunks. A famous tree called *"Il Gigante"* is 2,000 years old!

But even in the Cinque Terre, there is a machine that helps work on the steep slopes. The trenino is a monorail train which is used to transport tools, grapes and olives. There are about 50 trenino lines in this beautiful area; too bad we cannot use it as a panorama train.

Officially, no people can travel on the trenino but with us they made an exception. So after so many years, I finally travelled on the trenino and it was so much fun!

The olives are usually taken to the olive press (*frantoio*) within 24 hours. These presses are usually modern and not very nice. Unfortunately, we did not make it to an old, traditional olive mill. There is an old olive mill in Groppo(*antico frantoio*), owned by the National Park but it's been closed for a while. Of course, even in a modern press, it's very interesting to see how olives turn into olive oil. In Tuscany, we went to the press of Fattoria Montecchio near San Donato in Poggio while in Liguria we visited the Lucchi & Guastalli frantoio, in S. Stefano di Magra near La Spezia. In both places, the atmosphere was great, farmers kept arriving with their olives, and they were waiting for their new oil patiently but excited, chatting and laughing with the other farmers.

All farmers have an appointment with the press and they pay 15-22 EUR/100 kg. Olives arrive together with the leaves so the machine first seperates the leaves by blowing them away. Then the olives are washed thoroughly. Once they are clean, they go to the actual press machine where the pulp and the seeds are ground. Following this, the oil is extracted from the paste by centrifugation. It is important that extra virgin olive oil is made with cold pressing, under 27°C, only by mechanical method without the use of any chemicals.

When the fresh extra virgin olive oil appears, the owner has the right to taste it first. There's no hassle, they just use their small finger. The farmer then takes home the oil and the family tastes it right away with fresh bread and bruschetta.

It's interesting that olives are picked when they are not completely ripe. Ripe olives are purple. A green, not ripe olive will give less oil but it has a lower acidity level so the oil will be more fresh, more delicious and of better quality. In the case of extra virgin olive oil, there is a law that the acidity level cannot be more than 0.8%. Between 0.8% and 2%, it's a virgin olive oil. In the case of the world famous west-ligurian olive oil, Taggiasca, this level is around 0.03-0.05%.

Usually, more different olive types are mixed. If an oil is made of one kind of olive only, it's called monocultivar and it is more expensive. The D.O.P. sign on the bottles is also important. It means Denominazione di Origine Protetta: from protected origins. If you see this, you can be sure that the oil comes only from a certain territory. In Liguria, there are 3 different Riviera Ligure D.O.P. extra virgin olive oils: Riviera dei Fiori, Riviera del Ponente Savonese, Riviera del Levante. The Cinque Terre belongs to this last one. D.O.P. products are controlled very seriously. Cesare makes D.O.P. and simple extra virgin olive oils as well.

In Italy, families make their own oil or they buy from someone they know personally. This might seem like an exotic thing to do but in Italy making your own olive oil is as normal as making your own strawberry jam.

Good quality olive oil is not only delicious but also very healthy. If you go to Tuscany or the Cinque Terre, I recommend that you take some oil home with you. From this trip, we got home with about 15 liters of fresh olive oil. I use it every day but I hope it will last until next spring. Olive oil has to be stored in dark bottles in a cool and dark place so it will keep its quality for about 1.5 years.

In the Cinque Terre, we bought oil in the shop of the Cooperativa near Groppo and in the store of Cesare called Burasca on the main street of Manarola. I usually buy bigger quantities of the oil of the Lucchi & Guastalli frantoio at the market of La Spezia.

If you would like to see an olive harvest, plan your trip for November. I can help you find out the exact dates. In November, I can also handle accommodation booking flexibly, changing dates if needed. Colours and lights are beautiful this time of the year and if you are lucky, you will have nice warm autumn weather. We were sunbathing on the beach in a single t-shirt. In November, you will find hardly any tourists in the villages and accommodation prices are the lowest. So it's a great time to travel anyway.

Focaccia

Focaccia is basically a flat type of bread which is popular all over Italy. It seems similar to pizza but if you talk to Italians and tell them that focaccia is like pizza, they will object intensely. In Liguria, you will find the focaccia genovese with holes, simply seasoned with olive oil and salt. Of course, there are several versions with different toppings: vegetables, ham, cheese or herbs. Very famous is the focaccia di Recco which is filled with cheese. The people of Genova eat focaccia also for breakfast, dipping it into cafe latte.

Recipe for 4 people

- ✓ 500 g flour

- ✓ 1 cube yeast

- ✓ 1 cup lukewarm water

- ✓ 1 cup olive oil

- ✓ salt

Proof the yeast by combining it with the lukewarm water, add the flour and knead until the dough is smooth and elastic. Cover it and let it rise in a warm place for 1 hour. Rub olive oil in a baking pan, then spread the dough in the pan simply with your fingers until it is about 2 cms thick. Punch some holes in it (also with your fingers) and sprinkle coarse sea salt into the holes. Cover it with a damp towel and leave it for another 2 hours. In the end, sprinkle with some olive oil and bake it in a preheated oven at 220°C for 20 minutes.

Focaccia can be round, triangular, square, as you like it. It matches well with the white wines of Cinque Terre.

Pesto (basil sauce)

The Italian Riviera is the home of pesto, as the basil, the base of pesto, really likes the local climate. Basil is mixed with parmigiano (parmesan cheese), garlic, olive oil and pine nut. You can eat it on pasta, gnocchi, focaccia or pizza, but I also love it on a simple toast. Local people eat it mainly on a pasta called trofie.

You can buy freshly made pesto in the little shops of the Cinque Terre. However, I have found the best pesto at the market in La Spezia. If you walk down in the middle, the first stand on the left is called "Da Valerio". I love buying pesto and cheese here. It is also cheaper than in the 5 villages. At the market, a kilo of pesto costs approx. 16 EUR while in some little shops of the villages I've seen it for more than 40 EUR. You should also try the walnut sauce. I warn you, if you go to this market, you will end up with a basket full of delicious stuff.

Of course if you feel like it, you can also make your own pesto from fresh ingredients.

Recipe for 5 people

✓ 100 g basil

✓ 30 g pine nut

- ✓ 2 cloves of garlic

- ✓ 40 g parmesan cheese

- ✓ 2 dl olive oil

- ✓ Salt

Real pesto is made by hand in marble mortar with a wooden pestle but of course a mixer will also do.

Crush up basil, pine nuts and garlic with some salt in a mortar. Then mix with grated parmesan cheese and olive oil.

If you don't feel like cooking during your holiday, don't worry, you will find pasta with pesto and focaccia with pesto all around the Cinque Terre villages.

Other Information

Wedding in Italy

If you would like to have a special wedding on the Italian Riviera or in Tuscany, I am happy to help you with the organisation. You can have the ceremony in the villages of the Cinque Terre, Levanto or Portovenere, while in Tuscany there are many beautiful locations. As everyone has different ideas about the big day, we will plan the program and discuss all the details according to your wishes. Let me share with you the photos of Virág and Janó, as well as Réka and

Vilmos, who got married in the Cinque Terre and also spent part of their honeymoon here.

Virág and Janó

Virág and Janó almost had to cancel their wedding, as Virág hurt her knee just a few days before the big day. In the end they decided to be brave and adventurous and they had a really fun time in the Cinque Terre. Their wedding was in Levanto, and they stayed at a beautiful farmhouse in Levanto. They had a photographer with them for 3 days and took many photos not just at the wedding, but also before and after, in different locations. The Via dell'Amore was still open, so they could place their love lock there. They also trashed a dress on the beach of Monterosso, which they really enjoyed.

Réka and Vilmos

We faced several difficulties while organising the wedding of Réka and Vilmos but in the end, it all worked out perfectly. They got married at the Town Hall of Riomaggiore, on the balcony, with the view of the village and the sea. The ceremony was short and casual, but they love that about Italy. After the wedding they spent more time in Riomaggiore, then traveled to Pisa and Firenze to continue their honeymoon. When they got home they surprised the whole family with the news that it was not just a simple holiday...

Anniversary, birthday, marriage proposal

I've helped organise so many surprises in the past few years that by now, it has become a special service. I have to admit that these are my favourite projects! I love being part of a secret "plot" and set up a surprise in the Cinque Terre for someone who does not even suspect anything.

For some people the entire trip is a surprise, for a couple we had to make sure the apartment is big enough, as their friends joined them later, unexpectedly. A young man rented a sailboat to propose his girlfriend, while another man in love ordered a huge bunch of roses for their wine tasting. A gentleman surprised the newlyweds with a full-day boat rental, a fun girl took her best friend to the Cinque Terre for her 40th birthday and we organised several gastronomical programs for them.

My favourite was a couple who renewed their wedding wows in the church of Vernazza. So, the location is here, beautiful and romantic, now we just have to choose the right tour or other kind of surprise. All this on the quiet, of course. I believe that an experience in the Cinque Terre is worth more than diamonds!

Transfer

The Italian train system is very good, and you can easily get to the Cinque Terre by train. However, you might want more comfort, maybe you have heavy luggage or the train timetable does not match your flight departure or arrival time. In situations like these, I can offer you a private transfer to and from the Cinque Terre. You will have a private driver, and you will travel by car, minibus or bus, depending on the number of people. I get most requests for Pisa - Cinque Terre, Milan - Cinque Terre, Livorno - Cinque Terre and Rome - Cinque Terre transfers, but sometimes people just want to travel on to Portofino, Genova or Firenze in a comfortable way. If you would like to book a private transfer, please let me know how many people are travelling, how much luggage you are going to have and the exact date and time. I will send you the type of the vehicle I recommend and the exact price.

If you would like to hike in the area and get your luggage transported from village to village, I can also offer you luggage transfer. Please send me an e-mail with your hiking plans and I will send you the offer for the luggage transfer

Incentive tours in the Cinque Terre

With 15 years of experience in tourism and with my local knowledge I can help you organise custom-made incentive tours and team buildings for groups of all sizes. The Cinque Terre is an ideal destination as there are so many fun activities to choose from. You can combine hiking on breathtaking trails, sailing, a sunset tour, sea kayaking, cooking lessons and wine tastings, all this in a unique location. A fantastic trip to the Cinque Terre will surely inspire and motivate your team. Bring your colleagues to Italy and let them enjoy sunshine, sea, Mediterranean village life, delicious food and nice local wines in a stunning location. Tours are also possible in other parts of Liguria as well as in Tuscany.

Cinque Terre Card

Given the fact Cinque Terre is listed as a UNESCO site and that it is a protected area under the auspices of the National Park of Cinque Terre, mass tourism is carefully supervised as to its possible consequence of damaging the historical and nature patrimony of Cinque Terre. This is one of the reasons why Cinque Terre is often deemed a quaint destination, and this is one of the core coordinates in which the specific charm of the place resides.

The *Cinque Terre Card* was conceived by the authorities in charge with the management of the National Park of Cinque Terre in order to both protect the historical and nature patrimony of the region and to provide tourists with a useful tool while exploring the park. There are three versions of this card: the basic card, the train card and the ferry card. Except for the latter, the first two are valid for 1, 3 or 7 days, prices varying according to their validity period. The ferry card is issued for one day only.

The basic card allows visitors to use sundry public transport means and to gain access to various tourist sights: the hiking trail number 2 (commonly referred to as the blue trail), the Sciacchetra Museum in Manarola, the Oil Mill in Groppo, the Memory Museum in Riomaggiore, the Multimedia Hall in Levanto and to the observatory in Torre Guardiola. Moreover, owners of a basic Cinque Terre Card can also benefit from substantial discounts in the event they want to rent a bike from one of the tourist information offices in order to experience Cinque Terre on two wheels. On top of that, they can also enjoy significant discounts if they want to buy items from the shops of the National Park of Cinque Terre.

The train Cinque Terre Card guarantees users the same privileges of the basic card plus unlimited train travels on the Levanto-La Spezia line, of course, for the duration of the validity period of the card. Finally, the ferry Cinque Terre Card resumes the advantages of the previous two cards plus it allows visitors to use unlimitedly the ferries between the five Cinque Terre villages (except for Corniglia, which is a landlocked location) for the duration of one day (which coincides with the validity period of the card).

All the three types of Cinque Terre Cards can be purchased from any of the tourist information offices within the National Park of Cinque Terre. The prices, as said, vary according to the validity period and to the chosen type of card.

Cinque Terre Airports

A far as foreign tourists as concerned (but not exclusively), flying to Cinque Terre is the most time saving manner of making the trip. The region proper is serviced by no airport, but the airports pertaining to major cities in the surroundings of Cinque Terre are definitely a solution at hand. Thus, the Genoa Airport and the Pisa Airport are the first alternatives that can be taken into account, chiefly because the distance between each of them and Cinque Terre is, though around 100 kilometers, easily coverable by the airport transfer means.

Genoa Cristoforo Colombo Airport

Genoa Airport is located some 6 kilometers northwest of the city of Genoa, and about 110 kilometers from Cinque Terre. Built on an artificially created peninsula, the airport is serviced by both international and national airline companies which operate low-cost and business class flights alike. Thus, Alitalia, Belle Air, British Airways, Ryanair, Air France, Lufthansa and the rest of the companies provide connections with cities like Paris, Munich, Istanbul, Barcelona, Rome and London, ensuring a considerable tourist openness for the entire Ligurian region.

In terms of facilities and services, the airport is fitted for the needs of the people with reduced mobility, it offers a range of shopping opportunities and it is home to several car rental companies which enhance the airport transfer means for passengers who land at Cristoforo Colombo Airport.

Name:

Address:	Cristoforo Colombo, Sestri Ponente, Genoa, Italy
Telephone	0039 010 6015461
Fax	0039 010 6015487
Email:	info@airport.genova.it
Website:	www.airport.genova.it

Airport transfers from Genoa Cristoforo Colombo Airport to Cinque Terre

In order to reach Cinque Terre from Genoa Airport, tourists have to chief options: to drive to Cinque Terre or to resort to the public transport means. In the first case, getting to the A 12 Motorway, which is the main thoroughfare leading to Cinque Terre, is not complicated at all. Passengers only need to get to the A 10 Motorway, then take the A 7 Motorway, head north for some two kilometers and then finally turn east on the A 12 Motorway. Autostrada Azzura must be followed until visitors reach Carrodano, from where they must rely on the regional roads which meander throughout the National Park of Cinque Terre.

A less troublesome manner is to resort to the public transport means. In order to do that, tourists must first take the bus in order to get to the Genova Brignole Train Station and then take the train in the La

Spezia direction. The bus which ensures the connection between the airport and Genoa is operated by AMT, the public transport company of Genoa, and the service is called Volabus. Tickets can be purchased from the bus or from the airport.

For complete details on the bus shuttle from the airport to the Genoa Train Station (bus schedule, *ticket prices*, bus trip duration, stations and the like), use the information below:

Name:	AMT (Azienda Mobilita e Trasporti)
Address:	2, Via Montaldo, Genoa, Italy
Telephone:	0039 010 558114 / 0039 800 085311
Fax:	0039 010 5582400
Website:	www.amt.genova.it

For the complete list of trains which cover the Genoa-La Speza line, visit Trenitalia [www.trenitalia.com]. The regional trains are the only ones which stop in each of the five villages in Cinque Terre, which is why tourists must make sure they get in the right train or learn about the change trains by visiting the abovementioned official website of Trenitalia.

Pisa Galileo Galilei International Airport

Pisa Galileo Galilei International Airport is one of the most important airports in Tuscany, next to the airport in Florence. It is also one of the largest, being served by 18 airline companies (Lufthansa, Wizz Air, Ryanair, British Airways, Alitalia and Air France, just to count a few) which link Pisa and, by extension, the entire Tuscany, with destinations like Paris, Athens, London, the Canary Islands, Amsterdam and Bucharest.

The airport is fitted for the needs of the disabled and of the people with reduced mobility, and it also features a rewarding range of shopping opportunities and several bars and restaurants. The car rental companies which operate at the airport add to the list of airport transfer means, just as the taxis outside the terminals do.

The Pisa Galileo Galilei International Airport is located some 85 kilometers from Cinque Terre.

Name:	Pisa Galileo Galilei International Airport (Aeroporto Galileo Galilei) (PSA / LIRP)
Address:	Piazzale d'Ascanio, Pisa, Italy
Telephone:	0039 800 018849
Website:	www.pisa-airport.com

Airport transfers from Pisa Galileo Galilei International Airport to Cinque Terre

Pisa Galileo Galilei International Airport has excellent transfer alternatives for passengers who head for Florence. But as far as the tourists who intend to reach Cinque Terre, the most reliable solution refers to a combination of means of transport. Thus, they must get the bus to the Pisa Train Station and then head for Cinque Terre by train. For an even more straightforward alternative, tourists can get a train from the train station which is located near the airport, and make directly to Cinque Terre. For complete information on the trains between Pisa and Cinque Terre, visit Trenitalia.

For information on the buses which cover the distance between Pisa International Airport and the Pisa Central Train Station, schedules, ticket prices and the like, follow the indications below:

CPT (Compagnia Pisana Trasporti)

Name:	CPT (Compagnia Pisana Trasporti)
Address:	1, Via Bellatalla, Ospedaletto, Pisa, Italy
Telephone:	0039 800 570530 / 0039 800 012773 / 0039 050 884111
Fax:	0039 050 884284
Website:	www.cpt.pisa.it

In case driving to Cinque Terre is opted for by passengers who land at Pisa International Airport, they must take the A 12 Motorway and head north, then turn south west in order to reach La Spezia, from where the road infrastructure might come as a disappointment given is consists of narrow meandering thoroughfares which hinder the traffic.

Weather and Climate

Cinque Terre is located between the Ligurian Sea and the Apennine Mountains, a geographical situation which generates wholesome climatic conditions, at least from a tourist point of view. The impact of the Ligurian Sea breeze is noticeable during the winter season, when temperatures are mitigated by the sea influence, such that the average air temperatures stabilize around 12 degrees Celsius.

The mountains, on the other hand, shelter the region against the seasonal north winds, but the sea too has its major contribution to the air movement profile of Cinque Terre. Thus, the overall climate of the region can be best described as mild and warm, though the air temperatures tend to stabilize to an average value of 30 degrees Celsius in July and August, a feature which can hardly be considered mild.

Without being a dry area, Cinque Terre does not experience a large amount of rainfall, though abundant short-lasting showers do occur in spring and autumn. Given these considerations, it is obvious that late spring and early autumn are the best moments to visit Cinque Terre. July and August remain, however, the peak tourist season months, when crowd flock to Cinque Terre in order to explore its stunning opportunities.

The following links provide the 7-day weather forecast for each of the five major resort of Cinque Terre, taking into account several essential parameters: air temperature, humidity, rainfall, wind velocity, and UV values.

Tourist Information Offices in Cinque Terre

In Cinque Terre proper and in its surroundings there are several tourist information offices able to guide visitors during their stay on the Ligurian coast in respect to the accommodation solutions they can resort to, to the main itineraries they can search out, to the Cinque Terre Card and to sundry other tourist opportunities they can explore at leisure.

The authorities in charge with administrating the National Park of Cinque Terre are headquartered in Riomaggiore (the southernmost resort in Cinque Terre), but they also manage offices in plenty other localities in the region. Other resorts have information offices run by the local authorities. However, the entire Ligurian coast is dotted with tourist information offices, which is highly reassuring for people who want to extend their exploration of the national park by making the experience of the entire Ligurian Riviera.

Riomaggiore Tourist Information Office (Main Office)

Name:	Riomaggiore Tourist Information Office (Main Office)
Address:	26, Piazza Rio Finale, Riomaggiore, Italy
Telephone:	0039 0187 920633
Fax:	0039 0187 760092
Email:	info@parconazionale5terre.it
Website:	www.parconazionale5terre.it

Manarola Tourist Information Office (Administrative and Technical Office)

Name:	Manarola Tourist Information Office (Administrative and Technical Office)
Address:	Train Station, Manarola, Italy
Telephone:	0039 0187 762600 / 0039 0187 762640 / 0039 0187 760511
Fax:	0039 0187 760040
Email:	ufficio.tecnico@parconazionale5terre.it / accoglienzamanarola@parconazionale5terre.it
Website:	www.parconazionale5terre.it

Vernazza Tourist Information Office

Name:	Vernazza Tourist Information Office
Address:	Train Station, Vernazza, Italy
Telephone:	0039 0187 812533
Fax:	0039 0187 812546
Email:	accoglienzavernazza@parconazionale5terre.it
Website:	www.parconazionale5terre.it

Monterosso Tourist Information Office

Name:	Monterosso Tourist Information Office
Address:	Train Station, Monterosso, Italy
Telephone:	0039 0187 817059
Fax:	0039 0187 817151
Email:	accoglienzamonterosso@parconazionale5terre.it
Website:	www.parconazionale5terre.it

Corniglia Tourist Information Office

Name:	Corniglia Tourist Information Office
Address:	Train Station, Corniglia, Italy

Telephone:	0039 0187 812523
Fax:	0039 0187 812900
Email:	accoglienzacorniglia@parconazionale5terre.it
Website:	www.parconazionale5terre.it

Framura Tourist Information Office

Name:	Framura Tourist Information Office
Address:	41, Via Setta, Framura, Italy
Telephone:	0039 0187 823004 / 0039 0187 823053
Fax:	0039 0187 823071
Email:	iat@comune.framura.sp.it
Website:	www.comune.framura.sp.it

Levanto Tourist Information Office

Name:	Levanto Tourist Information Office
Address:	4, Piazza Mazzini, Levanto, Italy
Telephone:	0039 0187 808125
Email:	info@comune.levanto.sp.it
Website:	www.comune.levanto.sp.it

Bonassola Tourist Information Office

Name:	Bonassola Tourist Information Office
Address:	Via F.lli Rezzano, Bonassola, Italy
Telephone:	0039 0187 813500
Fax:	0039 0187 813529
Email:	info@prolocobonassola.it
Website:	www.prolocobonassola.it

Deiva Marina Tourist Information Office

Name:	Deiva Marina Tourist Information Office
Address:	Lungomare C. Colombo, Deiva Marina, Italy
Telephone:	0039 0187 815858 / 0039 0187 826136
Fax:	0039 0187 815800
Email:	ufficioturistico@comune.deivamarina.sp.it
Website:	www.comune.deivamarina.sp.it

Shopping in Cinque Terre

Shopping is not necessarily a tourist trump Cinque Terre can boast of, or, at least, Cinque Terre is not the most appealing destination for fashion victims, for instance. Yet while the mainstream shopping opportunities are close to nothing, tourists can definitely shop for the local traditional produces. Thus, the locally produced wines and olive oils, as well as the folk art works, stand out as a height of the regional shopping opportunities. Monterosso al Mare is where shopping in Cinque Terre is the most rewarding.

Enoteca Internazionale

Enoteca Internazionale is located in *Monterosso al Mare*, in the very center of the village, and it is, in fact, more than a mere wine shop (the oldest one in Monterosso, for that matter). It often organizes sampling events where the participants can indulge in wine and food tasting. While wines (international, national and regional alike) and liquors are the most prized products on sale, tourists might also be tempted to explore the range of olive oils, cheeses and traditional products showcased in this shop.

Name:	Enoteca Internazionale
Address:	62, Via Roma, Monterosso al Mare, Italy
Telephone:	0039 0187 817278
Fax:	0039 0187 817278
Email:	info@enotecainternazionale.com
Website:	www.enotecainternazionale.com

Vineria U Pussu

Vineria U Pussu is a venue not to be missed out by the dainty feeders who want to sample what is truly and genuinely specific about the local gastronomic and oenological offer. Ranging from exquisite wines to salted anchovies, the products proudly showcased by Vineria U Pussu entice visitors to delight into the most mouthwatering pursuit.

Name:	Vineria U Pussu
Address:	Via XX Settembre, Monterosso al Mare, Italy
Telephone:	0039 0187 817575

Cantina Cinque Terre / Societa Agricola Cooperativa

Located in the southernmost resort in Cinque Terre, namely, in *Riomaggiore*, Cantina Cinque Terre is a definite stop on the gastronomic tour of the region. It gathers all the specific flavors of the region, tempting tourists with the historical wines and the traditional olive oils and salted anchovies. A dreamlike place for visitors never tired of new gastronomic and oenological experiences.

Name:	Cantina Cinque Terre / Societa Agricola Cooperativa
Address:	Localita Groppo, Riomaggiore, Italy
Telephone:	0039 0187 920435
Fax:	0039 0187 920076

Email:	info5t@cantinacinqueterre.com / info@pec.cantinacinqueterre.com
Website:	www.cantinacinqueterre.com

Enoteca Sotto l'Arco

Enoteca Sotto l'Arco is located in *Vernazza* and, it too, stands out as an ideal opportunity to try out the strongest flavors of the local produces. The wines and the olive oils are complemented by the legendary pesto sauce which is one of the most representative gastronomic products of Cinque Terre.

Name:	Enoteca Sotto l'Arco
Address:	70, Via Roma, Vernazza, Italy
Telephone:	0039 0187 812124
Fax:	0039 0187 812124
Email:	info@enotecasottolarco.it
Website:	www.enotecasottolarco.it

Nightlife in Cinque Terre

Nightlife is not necessarily the most rewarding tourist pastime one can indulge in while spending their vacation in Cinque Terre. Most of the nocturnal buzz revolves around an extended diner while watching the sunset. We speak of a rather quaint pastime, with little dancing and clubbing opportunities, which, on the other hand, goes hand in hand with the idea of a vacation the satisfactions of which are yielded by the daytime pursuits.

Yet, for a taste of the most intense nocturnal opportunities, however canny they might be, tourists should turn to Monterosso al Mare and to Riomaggiore, where the kick comes down to several bars popular with tourists who search out the Ligurian coastline.

Bar La Conchiglia

Apart from the part Bar La Conchiglia is one of the few nightlife venues in Romaggiore, it is also one of the best rated. The chief advantage of this bar is it is located in a scenic set, with seaside view, in the vicinity of the harbor, a feature greatly prized by clients in search of unforgettable Ligurian sunsets. The bar also served light snacks.

Name:	Bar La Conchiglia
Address:	149, Via San Giacomo, Riomaggiore, Italy
Telephone:	0039 0187 920947

Bar Centrale

Bar Centrale is another notable option for people who want to relax with drink on the table while trying to charge their batteries after a hiking or sunbathing day. The bar is located in the center of *Riomaggiore*, and it is highly popular with tourists.

Name:	Bar Centrale
Address:	144, Via Cristoforo Colombo, Riomaggiore, Italy
Telephone:	0039 0187 920208

Il Casello

If beer and sunset is one's idea of perfect night out, then Il Casello is the ideal place for the most successful outcome of a nocturnal pastime in Cinque Terre. The bar is located in *Moneterosso al Mare*, and is stand for what is most representative of a typical Ligurian pub where nothing spectacularly happens, except for the fact it gives visitors the opportunity to indulge in the most pleasant moment of relaxation on the ever so demanding Ligurian coast.

Name: Il Casello

Addess: 70, Lungo Ferrovia, Monterosso al Mare, Italy

Fast
Fast is where tourists can the *cheapest beer* in town. This is, indeed, a virtue, since drinking the night out most of the time makes for an excellent tourist pastime. The bar also serves breakfast and lunch, though on the lighter side of the gastronomic spectrum.

Name: Fast

Address: 13, Via Roma, Monterosso al Monte, Italy

Traditional Cuisine in Cinque Terre

Much of the tourist industry in Cinque Terre revolves around the celebrated hiking trails of the namesake National Park. Yet, if truth be told, there's much more to Cinque Terre than hiking. Dainty feeders might find it comforting to learn Cinque Terre is a *gastronomic paradise*, accommodating in particular the fancies of fish and seafood dish lovers who know how to duly appreciate the gifts of the sea.

On top of that, the locally produced *wines* are, due to their historical reputation, a tourist magnet too. They can easily complement a meal and, if appropriately associated with a specific dish, they can make for a great culinary experience.

Traditional produces and dishes in Cinque Terre

Pesto

Pesto is a *garlic-based sauce*, but though garlic is, indeed, an essential ingredient, the specific garlic flavor is mitigated, so to say, by the mouthwatering bouquet yielded by the rest of the ingredients: pine nuts, basil, extra virgin olive oil and hard cheese. Pesto is, in fact, a product the tradition of which goes back to the Roman era, and its popularity is ascertained by the fact the entire Ligurian region delights in preparing and consuming it. Pesto is also commonly known as pesto alla Genovese, mainly because the historical recipe involves the use of Genovese basil, said to have a particular unique flavor.

In preparing the sauce, a special emphasis is laid on the fact it is not cooked, meaning the ingredients are not subject to any thermal alteration process. They are simply crushed, traditionally in a marble mortar and ground with a wooden pestle. This is a mechanical process which does not tamper with the genuine flavors of the ingredients, but preserves their entire sap such as to finally make the palate tremble with pleasure.

Pesto can accompany or enrich a large range of dishes, from soups to pasta.

Olive oil
The entire Ligurian region is famed for its traditional production of olive oil. The quality of the product is ascertained, amongst others, by the fact three of the types of olive oil have been granted the Ligurian Riviera Protected Designation of Origin (DOP) label, which ensures the authenticity of the product and guarantees its *high standard quality*.

The olive oil is a highly versatile ingredient, and not only gastronomically speaking, but also from a medical point of view, not to mention the wide range of beauty care products based on this chief active ingredient. Thus, there is a genuine olive oil culture in the Ligurian region of Italy, and visitors can ascertain it immediately after setting foot on the coast: the entire region is covered with olive groves and vineyards, providing not only a spectacular view, but also the prospect of inexhaustible gastronomic and oenological pursuits.

Salted anchovies

It's true fish is ever-present on locals' tables. Ranging from bream and bass to cuttlefish and squid, and boiled or salted, dried, fried or grilled, fish and seafood are a virtually unlimited source of inspiration for the local cuisine. However, the salted anchovies have become a mark of the regional cuisine, and, despite the fact this is not a spectacular dish, it does manage to fuel the already flamboyant imagination of keen dainty feeders.

Anchovies in general can be cooked in a variety of ways: fried and associated with vegetables (potatoes, for instance), brined, drowned in garlic sauce enriched with sundry herbs, or, why not, raw with olive oil and lemon juice. Either way, the anchovies are a must-try on the gastronomic tour of both Cinque Terre and of the entire Ligurian coastline.

Wines in Cinque Terre

The wholesome climate and soil of Cinque Terre have created the ideal conditions for olive cultures, but the land is also famed for its vineyards. There are two DOC labels originated here, namely, the *Cinque Terre wine* and the *Sciacchetra wine*. Unsurprisingly, the white Cinque Terre goes very well with fish and seafood dishes, whereas the sweet Sciacchetra is blends in very well with the dessert. A particular feature of Sciacchetra is it is made of dried grapes, which is precisely what gives the wine its specific sweetness.

Dining out in Cinque Terre

Tratoria La Lanterna
Tratoria La Lanterna is located right in the proximity of the Riomaggiore marina, which is why it offers clients the occasion to complement their gastronomic experience with the stunning view of the sea. The menu is fairly miscellaneous, but the seafood dishes are the tourists' favorites since the restaurant is said to keep close to the old traditions of preparing the recipes. Pasta is also appreciated. As if to enhance even more the appeal of the restaurant, the prices are quite reasonable. Reservations are advisable.

During the warm season, tables are available on the outdoor terrace.

Name:	Tratoria La Lanterna
Address:	46, Via S. Giacomo, Riomaggiore, Italy
Telephone:	0039 0187 920589
Fax:	0039 0187 24581
Website:	www.lalanterna.org

Tratoria Gianni Franzi
Tratoria Gianni Franzi is, by far, the most popular eating venue in Vernazza. Its success is guaranteed both by the restaurant's location and by the mouthwatering menu which mainly focuses on seafood and fish dishes. Tourists flock to Gianni Franzi precisely because the

cooks keep true to the ancient recipes which guarantee the excellence of the taste, of the flavor and of the texture. Briefly put, this is a Ligurian paradise where all palates with a craving for marine bouquets are welcomed with confidence. Reservations are highly advisable. During the tourist season, tables are arranged on the open-air terrace of the restaurant.

The owner of the restaurant also runs a *hotel in Vernazza*.

Name:	Tratoria Gianni Franzi
Address:	5, Piazza G. Marconi, Vernazza, Italy
Telephone:	0039 0187 821003
Fax:	0039 0187 812228
Email:	info@giannifranzi.it
Website:	www.giannifranzi.it

Ristorante Al Pozzo

Unsurprisingly, Ristorante Al Pozzo too excels in cooking and serving fish and *seafood specialties*. In fact, tourists often go there in order to sample the fresh catch, though pasta too is said to be excellent. Adding the ambiance and the set, it's no surprise Ristorante Al Pozzo is one of the most popular eating venues in Monterosso al Mare.

Name:	Ristorante Al Pozzo

Address:	4, Via Roma, Monterosso al Mare, Italy
Telephone:	0039 0187 817575
Website:	www.alpozzoristorante.it

Ristorante Miky

Ristorante Miky is a first class eating venue in Monterosso al Mare where not only the menu, but also the atmosphere, contributes to an unforgettable gastronomic experience. The restaurant is, it too, a top choice for tourists who want to sample the genuine flavors and tastes of the *Ligurian cuisine*. The salted fish is the restaurant's specialty, but the chef is also famed for his homemade pasta. A fine selection of wines, including the celebrated white Cinque Terre, complements the menu.

Name:	Ristorante Miky
Address:	104, Via Fegina, Monterosso al Mare, Italy
Telephone:	0039 0187 817608
Fax:	0039 0187 817608
Email:	miky@ristorantemiky.it
Website:	www.ristorantemiky.it

Ristorante Via Venti

Ristorante Via Venti welcomes its clients with a Ligurian menu, offering delightful regional and local dishes. The seafood selection is accompanied by a range of *pasta specialties*, all of these being highly appreciated by most of the tourists who stumble across the small Ristorante Via Venti. On top of that, this eating venue is highly appreciated for its location (on one of the oldest thoroughfares of Monterosso al Mare) and for the friendly welcoming staff.

Name:	Ristorante Via Venti
Address:	32, Via XX Settembre, Monterosso al Mare, Italy
Telephone:	0039 0187 818347
Fax:	0039 0187 818377
Email:	info@ristoranteviaventi.it
Website:	www.ristoranteviaventi.it

National Park of Cinque Terre

The *National Park of Cinque Terre* is just one of the many national parks of Italy. However, this is quite a special one, keeping in mind the fact that the region has been declared a national park in order to preserve the natural environment. Thus, since Cinque Terre has been altered by human intervention over the centuries, this National Park should be named The Park of Man, instead.

But why would it need such a labeling?

Over the times, starting the 10th century, man has dissected the hills that run into the sea in order to create arable land and indeed they created. Cinque Terre was renowned across the centuries for its olive and wine production. However, the landscape remained as beautiful as before, becoming even more appealing to man.

Nevertheless, modern times came and all those terraced hills were left on their own, degrading themselves. And, with degradation, came ugliness. This is, probably, the main reason why Cinque Terre was transformed first into a *UNESCO World Heritage* in 1997, and a national Park in 1999 these hills crashing into the sea were beautiful before man came. And, because man changed them irremediably, they should be kept changed, but they should be kept nonetheless.

Therefore, this should be named The Park of Man instead because this park's goal is to restore the balance, the lost harmony between man and nature. Because there are very few places that remained wild and were not tamed, if they remained at all.

As a result, the policy is that of a sustainable development tourism development that protects and enhances future opportunities, while also keeping present ones safe.

We might say that this national park has a profound identity in the region's culture whether we are talking about architecture or art in general, or we are talking about the olive and grapes culture. Therefore, it cannot exist without any of them, man or nature. And, if it is easier to keep man somewhere, it is more difficult to maintain what man has done over the centuries.

And this is this National Park's goal to make sure that both man and nature coexist, like they did for centuries, no matter what happens, no matter how modern times are shaped.

Getting there & around

Getting around by car

You will often hear that the Cinque Terre is car-free, you cannot enter the villages, you should not come by car, etc. Well, actually, it is only partly true. Most of the villages are really for walking only but you can enter in some areas. For example, you can drive through the central part of Corniglia or some areas of Monterosso. You can reach every village by car, park at the entrance of the villages and then walk from there.

Actually, I love driving around the Cinque Terre. For me, it's so much fun! The view from the road is stunning, the roads are winding through vineyards and olive groves so it's a really scenic drive. You can stop at several viewpoints to enjoy the amazing panorama.

The coastal road above the villages is comfortable for 2 cars in most places (see the photo above), and it's good quality. Then from this road, you will turn off onto smaller, narrow roads leading to each village. Those roads are really winding and at certain points you need to stop as there is room for one car only. You can see the road to Corniglia on the photo below. You may find it scary, I find it breathtaking.

At the same time, I have to admit that I hate to be a passenger in a car around here. Unfortunately, I get motion sickness on everything that moves, also in the car, unless I am driving. So sitting on the passenger seat on these roads for me is a nightmare. So I always hang on to the wheel...

To sum it up, don't worry and come by car if you are an experienced driver, if you don't mind narrow and winding roads, if you love driving on scenic coastal roads, if you don't mind spending your time looking for parking places and if your passengers don't get carsick. Otherwise, it's much better and easier to arrive by train. You car will be parked most of the time anyway so you can save on car rental costs and parking fees as well.

OK, so if you are arriving by car, you will be driving on one of the Italian motorways towards La Spezia. In La Spezia, you will turn onto the coastal road.

Important! At the moment, the coastal road in the middle is closed. To get to Riomaggiore, Manarola, Corniglia and Vernazza, you have to come this way, via La Spezia. But to get to Monterosso, you have to exit the highway at Levanto-Carrodano. Also, do not use the Brugnato exit as the road from there to the Cinque Terre is closed as well!

Parking in the villages of the Cinque Terre
It is true that you cannot enter the historical centre of the villages by car but you will find a car park in every village. These are partly protected but even if there is no guard around, you do not need to worry, the area is safe. Local inhabitants also park here. So you need to leave the car in the parking lot and walk or take the local green buses.

When you are looking for a parking space, pay attention to the colour of the lines. Yellow lines mean resident parking, blue lines mean paid parking for guests (see photo below) while white lines mean free parking.

Parking fees

Riomaggiore: 24 EUR/car/day
Parking in Riomaggiore is very expensive so it's better to arrive by train. If you have a car, you could park in another village and take the train from there, it only takes a few minutes. The parking area is at the entrance of the village, at the top of the main street. It's quite a walk up from the center and the sea. There is a green bus to and from the

center. There is a small office where you have to buy your parking ticket.

Manarola: 20 EUR/car/day

If you book a room or apartment in Manarola with me, I can help you book a garage in Manarola for 17 EUR/car/day. The number of garages is limited so please enquire well in advance. The garage is in the same area as the resident parking. When you first arrive in Manarola, you will come to a gate. The guest parking is before that gate. This gate is usually open between 7:00-10:00AM and 2:00-4:00PM so travellers can drive further down to Manarola to load or unload the luggages. In the tourist season, there is usually a person at the gate so even if it's closed, you can ask for a 20-minute permit to enter. But make sure you drive back up right away, and do not park in the resident parking area, otherwise you might get a fine.

There are usually free parking spaces further up along the road but watch out for the "no parking" signs, especially around the curves. You could also consider driving up to Groppo or Volastra. Parking is free there so you could leave the car there and take the bus down or walk down. Of course, check into your accommodation and unload your bags first.

Corniglia: 10 EUR/car/day

In Corniglia, quite a few accommodations have their own parking space in the village. So if you arrive by car, Corniglia can be a good choice for you. I can offer you several apartments with free parking. Otherwise, parking is along the road in Corniglia. There is a bigger parking area before you reach the village. And if all seems full, drive through the center and go further down towards the railway station, there are usually empty spots there. You have to buy your parking ticket from a machine. There are 2 machines, one at the parking area before the village, the other one just as you enter Corniglia, at the start of the walking path. You can get a daily ticket or also by the hour, you can switch between the 2 tariffs with the button at the top.

Vernazza: 12 EUR/car/day

The roads to Vernazza were badly ruined in the big floods a few years ago and still have not been fixed. I drove down to the village once and it was really scary, even for me. Even parts of the road were missing. So I do not recommend arriving to Vernazza by car. Park in Monterosso, Levanto or La Spezia instead and take the train to Vernazza. In case you really want to drive to Vernazza: the lower parking is for Vernazza's inhabitants only. You can drive down with your luggage, unpack, then take the car back to the upper parking. There are only about 60 parking spaces so you might not find a spot, especially on weekends and during the main season. From there, you can walk down about 1 km or you can take the local bus. UPDATE: I drove to Vernazza from the direction of Corniglia and that road was ok. I asked the person selling the parking tickets and he said this road is better than the one coming from the direction of Monterosso. So if you have to drive to Vernazza, better to arrive via La Spezia, turning off towards Corniglia, and then Vernazza. The problem is, this was in July and the parking was absolutely full.

Monterosso: 25 EUR/car/day
In Monterosso, there are two parking areas, one in the old town and another one in the new town, by the sea. Find out where your accommodation will be and choose the parking which is closer. When you are driving to Monterosso, at one point there will be an intersection. Turn right to go to Fegina or turn left for the old town (Centro storico). The Fegina parking is really big, it's right by the sea and quite close to the railway station. So it is also a good option if you are staying in other villages but prefer to park in Monterosso and take the train from there. In the historical center, just at the end of the pedestrian area, you will find the Loreto parking which is actually a parking house.

Levanto: 10.50 EUR/car/day
There is a large parking area right behind the railway station. You can pay with coins at the machine or at the railway station.

Groppo, Volastra: free
You can park in these villages even if you don't stay there, and walk down to Manarola or take the green bus. The villages are very small so parking spaces are limited. Also, please respect the area for resident parking and only use the spots marked with white lines.

La Spezia: 24 EUR/car/day or free.
There is a parking house right under the railway station so it is very comfortable. But there is also a free parking area in Piazza d'Armi, only a 10-minute walk to the railway station. As far as I know, there is also a shuttle bus to the railway station every 30 minutes in case you have big luggage. If you come to the Cinque Terre for one day and are planning to take the boat from La Spezia, you can find parking spaces right in front of the harbour.

Remember, wherever you park, you will still need to walk. In case of most accommodations, there will be steps as well. So here is a tip: pack light or have a strong man in your company.

And one more thing: I last checked the prices in July 2015, and they change from time to time. So prices can be a few euros higher when you arrive. If you notice any changes, please send me an email about it, I would really appreciate it.

Getting there by plane

If you are flying to Italy and looking for an airport close to the Cinque Terre, you have several options. In the list below, you can see how long it takes to get to Riomaggiore (by train) from your chosen airport. The train usually leaves from the central railway station so first you will have to get from the airport to the station.

✓ Pisa 1–1.5 hours

✓ Genoa 1.5–2 hours

✓ Florence 2.5–3.5 hours

✓ Milan 3.5–4 hours

✓ Rome 3.5–4.5 hours

✓ Nice 5–6 hours

✓ Venice 5–6 hours

Getting around by train

The easiest and fastest way to travel between the villages of the Cinque Terre is by train. The line connecting the 5 villages is part of the main Italian railway line between Rome and Genova so there is at least one train going in both directions every hour. Most trains stop in Riomaggiore, Monterosso, Levanto and La Spezia but only regional trains stop in Manarola, Corniglia and Vernazza. You can get a free printed timetable at the railway station in every village.

If you are just planning your trip and would like to check train timetables, you can do that on www.trenitalia.com. But don't look for Cinque Terre as you won't find it. You have to enter the name of one of the 5 villages. Sometimes, if you are planning well ahead of time, you won't find any trains for your dates. That's because those timetables are not uploaded yet. In this case try to search for a closer date. Most trains will be the same, but schedules do change by the season, so make sure you doublecheck closer to your travel date.

UPDATE 2016 MAY:

The Cinque Terre Express train has been introduced, which goes back and forth between La Spezia and Levanto, every 30 minutes. A single ticket costs 4 EUR for this train, which is ridiculously expensive, but there is nothing we can do about it. If you are planning to take the train several times a day, it's better to purchase the Cinque Terre Train Card.

Between the villages, the train travels in the tunnel most of the time, under the terraced hills so unfortunately you can't enjoy the beautiful view. It is important to know that sometimes trains (especially the long ones) stop partly in the tunnel but you still have to get off. I have seen many tourists hesitating or even staying on the train because of the strange stops. (Of course I helped them whenever I had a chance.) There are big signs for every village so if you pay attention, you can't miss your stop.

The journey between the villages only takes a few minutes:
- ✓ La Spezia Riomaggiore 9 minutes
- ✓ Riomaggiore Manarola 2 minutes
- ✓ Manarola Corniglia 4 minutes

✓ Corniglia Vernazza 5 minutes

✓ Vernazza Monterosso 5 minutes

✓ Monterosso Levanto 5 minutes

As there are only two platforms in the villages of the Cinque Terre, it is easy to find your way around. If you want to go towards Monterosso (and Levanto), you will have to follow the sign "PER GENOVA". If you travel towards Riomaggiore (and La Spezia), look for the "PER LA SPEZIA" sign. From the stations, you can usually see the sea which makes orientation even easier. If you are facing the sea, Monterosso, Levanto and Genova are to your right while Riomaggiore and La Spezia are to your left.

Arrivals and departures are shown on TV screens. Only the final destinations are shown which may be unknown, far away cities. At every railway station, you will find a large yellow poster on the wall with detailed information about all the trains. So you can see if the train going to a certain final destination will stop in the village where you want to go. You can also check how many stops the train will make and what is the last stop before your destination so you will surely get off at the right place. Arriving trains are shown on a large white poster.

There is another type of poster which may be useful if you travel to a faraway destination with an IC or Freccia train and you have prebooked seats. These trains can be very long and it is not funny to run from carriage 1 to carriage 9 with your backpack or suitcase, competing against the whistle of the conductor. On this poster, you can see which way the train will be going and where is carriage 1. Don't think that logically it is always right after the engine. You are in Italy!

By the way, another good advice if you are travelling around Italy by train. Once you figure out the right platform, take off your heavy backpack and comfortably sit down on a bench, don't think that you can relax. It happened quite a few times that with a group of 10 people we had to rush from one platform to the other, up and down many steps, because they kept changing the platform numbers. So always keep an eye on the TV screens and listen to the announcements.

It is a very important rule that you can never cross the tracks, you always have to use the underpass. Shouting railway employees and a possible penalty are not the only reason to keep this rule. In Italy, the fast trains don't even slow down, they simply speed through the stations. If you don't hear the announcement of the arriving train, it will surprise you. So don't ever walk on the tracks and always stand at least 2 meters from the rails, especially with children. You should never stand inside the yellow line.

Another important thing in Italy: you have to validate your ticket at the railway station with the automats before getting on the train. Regional tickets can be used any time so it will only be valid if the machine stamps the actual date on it. So only validate your ticket when you are actually going to use it. If you have a booked seat for a certain date, there is no need to validate but to be sure, I always did. If you don't have a validated ticket, you can get a serious fine, unless you convince the conductor with your beautiful smile. If you forget, and only realize when the train is already moving, look for the conductor, tell him you have forgot and ask them to validate. This always worked for me. Fines mean a serious income for Trenitalia (Italian Railways) as many tourists have no idea about this system.

If you travel by train in Italy, it is good to remember this word: SCIOPERO (strike). If you see or hear this world, you can expect some chaos. It is one of my "favourite" words; I had to face this challenge quite a few times. Strikes are often on Friday, this way they can have a nice long weekend. A strike does not mean there are no trains at all but there are only a few, on certain routes and with big crowds. In my experience, the employees sitting in the ticket office and the information booth take striking very seriously. They don't want to help and they insist that there are no trains running and I shouldn't even buy a ticket. I always insisted on buying my ticket, and although it took longer and sometimes I did not have a seat, I always managed to get to my destination. Of course, only try this if you are adventurous enough!

Watch your bags on the trains and at the railway stations. Unfortunately there are some thieves specialized in tourists. The sad thing is that they are often kids and young girls. So keep an eye on your backpack and never keep your wallet in your back pocket. If you are careful, you will be safe.

Getting around by boat

It is a wonderful experience to travel along the Cinque Terre coastline by boat. The villages look quite different if you look at them from the sea, and who doesn't enjoy sitting on a boat on a hot summer day?

There are public ferry boats running between the villages, but they are very crowded. So if you don't like the idea of taking the boat with hundreds of other tourists and are looking for a more relaxed experience

If you decide to take the public ferry, here is some information for you. The boats run between Monterosso and Portovenere (also La Spezia) both directions and stop in every village except Corniglia. You can also take a boat tour from Portovenere around the 3 islands or travel to Levanto, Lerici and Portofino.

Boats usually run between April 1 and October 31 but it also depends on the weather and sea conditions. In case of bad weather, boat service may be suspended any time.

You should also take the boat around the Portofino peninsula. Private boat rental is possible there as well!

Otherwise, there are 2 companies working in that area. The eastern side of the peninsula is called the Golfo del Tigullio and boats are running between San Fruttuoso, Portofino, Santa Margherita Ligure, Rapallo, Chiavari, Lavagna and Sestri Levante. They also have boats that run all the way to the Cinque Terre and back. For details, routes, schedules and prices, please check their website. Another company operates on the other side of the peninsula, in the Golfo Paradiso. You can take their boat from San Fruttuoso to Camogli but they have several different lines between Genova and Portofino, or even Genova and the Cinque Terre

Getting there by cruise

Going on a Mediterranean cruise has become extremely popular for the past few years. If you are planning one and you will board in Genova or La Spezia, you should consider spending a few days in the Cinque Terre before or after your cruise. In case you board somewhere else and your ship will stop in La Spezia or Portovenere, you probably want to spend a day in the Cinque Terre. The cruise companies offer day tours to the area. Those groups are usually quite large, around 50 people, and in my opinion it is not possible to enjoy the Cinque Terre in such a big group.

If you would like to have a more relaxed experience and a day tour planned especially for you, just send me an email. I can organise a personal guide for you in several languages and also private transfer if needed. I will help you create the best itinerary. We will take you to some off the beaten track places in the Cinque Terre, away from the crowds. Your local guide will explain why the Cinque Terre is such a unique place on earth. We can include a nice wine tasting with light lunch for you, as the wines of the Cinque Terre are really important in local life and history.

Getting around by bus

In the Cinque Terre National Park, the protection of the environment is of high importance so you can travel only in an environmentally friendly way in the villages. Besides trains and boats, electric buses are used, which run between the coast and the villages and sanctuaries higher above the hills.

You can use these buses free with the Cinque Terre Card, otherwise one ticket costs 2.50 EUR if you buy it on the bus and 1.50 EUR if you get it at the tourist information centers of the National Park. I think it is worth getting on these little buses: you can get to some smaller, quieter villages, like Groppo and Volastra, or you can visit some hidden churches. On the coastal road, where the buses run, you can enjoy an amazing view over the sea and the terraces. The drivers are usually local guides as well so they might tell you about local life and answer your questions.

In some villages, you can take the bus from the parking area to the center if you wouldn't like to walk a few minutes. In Corniglia, you can get by bus to the village center from the train station.

Please ask the Information Centers of the National Park for schedules.

The bus routes are:

✓ Riomaggiore Monesteroli Biassa Telegrafo

✓ Manarola Groppo Cantina Volastra

✓ Corniglia Stazione (railway station) Corniglia paese (center of the village)

✓ Vernazza Sant. Reggio Drignana Fornacchi S. Bernardino Murro Vernazzola

✓ Monterosso Santuario di Soviore

The combination of taking the bus and hiking is also a good way to discover the national park if you don't like tiring uphills. It is nice to walk down from the Telegrafo to Riomaggiore. Another great option is taking the bus from Manarola to Volastra, then hiking from Volastra to

Corniglia. You could also take the bus from Vernazza or Monterosso up to the sanctuaries and walk down from there. From Vernazza, just take a roundtrip with the bus to enjoy the great views. The view of Vernazza from the top of the hill is one of my favourites in all of the Cinque Terre. Although the drivers generally stop at the lookout point for a quick photo stop, it's always better to ask them. The buses are usually used by locals living further up the hills.

There is now a brand new bus service called "Explora 5 Terre" connecting the villages and some hamlets of the Cinque Terre. This small bus can be a very nice alternative to the crowded trains, especially that the views from the road are stunning. The buses have 22 seats, they have A/C and your driver will give you a small map of the route and the villages. The buses run between 8:30AM and 10:00PM, every day of the year.

Stops of the Explora buses

✓ La Spezia - La Spezia Centrale railway station

✓ La Spezia - Piazza Mercato

✓ Riomaggiore - Castello (above the castle)

✓ Riomaggiore - Lavaccio (at the top of Riomaggiore, near the roundabout)

✓ Manarola - Piazza della Chiesa (at the Church square)

- ✓ Groppo - Cantina Sociale (at the building of the Cinque Terre wine cooperative)

- ✓ Volastra

- ✓ San Bernardino

- ✓ Corniglia (on the main square)

- ✓ San Bernardino

- ✓ Vernazza (near the parking area)

At the moment the bus cannot go to Monterosso, as the road between the two villages is closed. On certain days the bus also stops in La Spezia at the cruise terminal.

Prices

- ✓ Explora one day pass, adults: 22 EUR.

- ✓ Explora one day pass, kids 4-12: 17 EUR.

- ✓ Explora one day pass, kids 0-3: free.

- ✓ Explora plus, combined pass with the one day Cinque Terre card: 26 EUR.

- ✓ Explora one day discounted price, if you are staying in an authorised accommodation of the Cinque Terre: 18.50 EUR.

Where Should I Stay?

Staying in one of the five villages means you don't have to travel in each day and can soak up the atmosphere in the evenings. But because it's so popular, accommodation is pricey even for pretty uninspiring places so try to book early. There aren't many hotels, only in the larger villages Monterosso and Riomaggiore, so it's mostly guesthouses and apartment rentals. The villages are so close together that there isn't one that's in a better position than the others. And it's not really worth moving around and staying in a couple of different villages as you can get between them so easily. It's more a case of picking the one which has the right sort of character for you (and where you can find somewhere decent that's within your budget!).

Monterosso's the furthest north and the largest of the villages. It's easiest to get to so gets busy, and is the only one with a proper beach and a seafront promenade. It's got the widest selection of accommodation and the best hotels, with more of a resort feel and it's the least hilly so is the most accessible. At the other end of the Cinque Terre is Riomaggiore, another of the larger villages with a gorgeous setting around the harbour. It's also got lots of places to eat and the best nightlife, but brace yourself for plenty of hills.

Vernazza and Manarola are smaller and arguably the most beautiful of the villages. Manarola is surrounded by vineyards and Vernazza has a tiny beach. Both have mostly self-catering accommodation. As does Corniglia, which is the smallest village and the hardest to get to, as there's no sea access and a huge flight of steps up to the village from the train station. This makes it the quietest especially in the evenings and its position high up on the rocks means you get some great views (this is where I stayed and loved it).

A cheaper option is to stay in neighbouring Levanto or La Spezia both are on the Cinque Terre train line but accommodation, food and pretty much everything are cheaper as you're not in the 'proper' Cinque Terre. You also have a bit more of an authentic, local feel as they're not quite so overrun with visitors.

How Hard Are the Walks?

For centuries the only way you could get between the Cinque Terre villages was on foot, and it's still the best way to get around, with a constant stream of gorgeous views. There's a mix of coastal and hill paths. Though the coast paths aren't just a walk along the seafront at least not the part that's open. The one flat stretch of coast path from Corniglia to Riomaggiore is closed for the foreseeable future after landslips damaged it back in 2011. The rest of the paths involve lots of ups and downs with some rocky ground and a few big drops and steps to clamber up. You don't need to be really fit but do need to be be comfortable walking uphill and have decent walking shoes most people were wearing hiking boots or sturdy trainers.

The distances involved aren't huge, but it can take longer than you'd guess from the distance as it's so hilly. Plus you often end up waiting for people to pass on narrow stretches which slows things down. So start early or late if you can to miss the peak of walkers. The Sentiero Azzurro or Blue Trail starts from Monterosso and takes around two hours to Vernazza and another two hours on to Corniglia. From Corniglia to Manarola you have to take the high route via Volastra it takes around three hours and involves some serious climbs but the views at the top through the vineyards are well worth it. Then from Manarola you can walk on to Riomagiorre via Beccara in around 90 minutes, though there's another big climb to start.

As well as the main walks there are lots of quieter hill paths, like the Sentiero Rosso or Red Trail from Portvenere to Levanto. There are also shorter sanctuary walks which run steeply up into the hills from the villages. And even if you're not hiking there's lots of hills, steps and walking in the villages too.

Do I Need a Permit?

To walk the coast path from Monterosso to Corniglia you need to buy a Cinque Terre Card. You can get them in the villages and from huts at the start of each section of the path. If you're walking between Corniglia and Riomaggiore you have to take the hill path so don't need a permit. The cards cost €7.50 for one day or €14.50 for two days.

They include free wifi, local buses and toilets (€1 otherwise). Or there's a train version which also includes unlimited train travel on the Cinque Terre line between Levanto and La Spezia. They cost €16 for one day, €29 for two or €41 for three, with discounts for children, families and off season.

How Long Should I Spend There?

If you're really tight on time you could 'do' the Cinque Terre in one day by starting super early and walking straight through from one end to the other. There are a lot of day trip tours available or you can just take the train or boat from one village to the next with an hour in each. But you wouldn't be really doing it justice, and you'd be missing out on the best time of day. Between 10am and 4pm the villages are rammed with day-trippers the train platform in Monterosso at 4pm took me right back to commuting on the Tube in London at rush hour. But come the evenings things calm right down and there's much more of a relaxed feel.

Ideally you'd want to spend three or four days in the Cinque Terre to do it justice. That'd give you enough time to explore each of the villages, do a couple of half-day walks and take a boat trip along the coast. The villages have a different atmosphere at different times of day, so that'd give you time to decide on your favourite so you can go back for sunset or dinner. And if you've get more time, there are plenty more walks to do, or you could travel further afield and visit neighbouring Portovenere, Levanto or La Spezia.

When's The Best Time to Visit the Cinque Terre?

I don't think the Cinque Terre is ever exactly quiet high season runs all the way from Easter until October. But to avoid the worst of the crowds, steer clear of July and August. Accommodation gets booked up really far in advance in summer and it can get really hot so isn't the best time for walking. Shoulder season May/early June and September is a good time to go, with warm days and less people. Or if you want to risk the off-season you can get a bargain and the paths to yourself, but it can be wet, especially around November. And if the weather's bad you risk the boats being suspended and the trails closed.

My Experience

"On the port of Vernazza, the lights were sometimes scratched by the rising of the invisible waves at the bottom of the night" (from "Le Occasioni", 1939) a scene Eugenio Montale loved to observe during the strong storms that filled the air with saltiness. The harsh and devious landscapes of Cinque Terre inspired Montale for his hermetic rhymes and gained him a Nobel Prize for Literature in 1975. Montale is just one of the poets, novelists and artists that got inspired by this amazing land.

Here is the story of how we enjoyed our staying in Cinque Terre, here is how we explored the nearby pearls Portovenere and Portofino and truly lived this magical land. Here is the story of how we got engaged

Monterosso is the western most village of the "five lands" (one land one village, basically). The remaining four (west to east) are Vernazza, Corniglia, Manarola and Riomaggiore. We took a train ride from Milan to Monterosso and it went easy and smooth. You can catch offers for 10€ if you are lucky and if you book well in advance. After arriving to Monterosso we had to get off and change to a local train that connects Cinque Terre every 20/30 minutes.

Train is the most convenient means of transport. You can buy a Cinque Terre Treno Card, which gives you access to all trains between Levanto Monterosso Vernazza Corniglia Manarola Riomaggiore La Spezia Centrale. When you buy the card in the tourist information point, they will also give you a time table of train departures keep it at reach as you hop on and off between the stations. Included in the cost of the card is the access to all hiking paths ("sentieri" in Italian) which connect the five villages.

If you are up for a bit more of adventure, hiking will give you a completely different perspective and a chance to truly explore the surrounding National Park.

When it comes to accommodation, we paid 120€ per night for the apartment (during July super high season); it's probably not a cheap option, unfortunately we booked a bit late and there wasn't so much to choose from. As the villages are small, booking well ahead is advised in case you want to have more affordable accommodation in Cinque Terre. An alternative is to stay slightly outside the area (e.g. in La Spezia) and then use the local train to reach your destination (its' not far).

Restaurant prices in Cinque Terre are about 10-14 euro for pasta or risotto dishes and 16-20 euro for meat and fish courses. If you are already familiar with Italian cuisine try to pick those places that offer "a taste of Liguria", order local dishes (for example "bagnun") to see and taste what they are like. It is always good to have cash with you as many places in Italy don't go well with credit cards.

When it comes to safety and security, we didn't feel any threats, despite the many warnings for pickpockets at the train stations.

And now, let's look into the different villages:

Our accommodation was in Corniglia, the highest of the five villages, built on top of a cape, with a breath-taking view of the Ligurian sea. The train station is almost at sea level, so in order to reach the village center you have 3 options:

➤ Take a mini-bus that runs approximately every 15 min between the station and the village center. The bad news is that there is no services later in the evening. The good news is that the cost of the ticket (1.5€) is included in the Cinque Terre Card!

➤ Walk the 300 and more steps that bring you almost at the village center. Of the two walking options this is probably the fastest, but it requires trained legs and lungs if you want to make it without running out of breath.

➤ Walk the same road that the shuttle bus takes. This is the longest option, however the road is not very steep, so it's probably the most suitable option for the less fit ones (and you also get a nice view of the local vineyards).

If you are in search of more authentic country-style feeling of Italy, then don't look no further and choose Corniglia among the five! You will have to cope with the tedious walks from the station of course, and learn how to sleep despite the church bell which rings throughout the night and gives you a kick-off salute at 7am (when the country-life in the vineyards is supposed to start). Surely the other 4 villages might be prettier and better fit for your Instagram killer-photo. But after a few days in Corniglia, the few families that run the local businesses become your own family, you get to know most of the locals and you get to meet Igor. Igor, the local dog that apparently everybody knows, will welcome you wagging his tail and when you fill his water bowl next to the drinking fountain, you will become his new friend.

First day CORNIGLIA

On our first day, we decided to spend the few hours left in the afternoon to visit one of the 3 nearby beaches, or maybe they better be called "points of access to the water". If you are expecting a long beach full of white and fine sand, surrounded by palm trees and coconuts, then you are probably reading the wrong review (check out our Caribbean Cruise article instead). One of the 3 beaches close to Corniglia, Guvano Beach, is unfortunately not accessible anymore, due to a landslide in 2011 that brought destruction in the area and irreversibly changed the landscape of Cinque Terre. The biggest of the 3 beaches, the one that is right behind the train station didn't seem so appealing (very narrow area with rocks and continuous noise from the trains). So we decided to go for the 3rd (and best) option...a cosy marina bay that is accessible through stairs from village center.

Like almost everything in Cinque Terre, the path to the bay requires a bit of trained legs and is not adjusted for strollers/wheelchairs, but your senses will be rewarded once you arrive.

We found this place lovely, with few people (given the high season) and with crystal clear water. Be aware though that getting into the water is not easy. We had to literally slide down some rocks in order to enjoy a swim. Here is a very important tip: if you plan to have a dip in the water every now and then in Cinque Terre, you must bring with you a pair of swimming shoes. They will make your life much easier by protecting your feet from the cutting edges of the stones and will provide you with that extra grip you need to move comfortably between the rocks. After a refreshing swim and a little shower to remove the salt, we let ourselves indulge in a beautiful sunset from the "comfort" of our rock. Needless to say the warmth of the colors are worth a few pictures and if you are on a romantic trip, your partner will surely fall deeper in love with you…it's a guarantee

Second Day: Vernazza & Monterosso

For our second day we had planned Vernazza and Monterosso as our destinations. We started the day with a generous breakfast in Corniglia, we bought some tasty "verdure ripiene" stuffed veggies and awesome-tasting tomatoes at a local shop called "A Bütiega" (you will see a lot of Ligurian spelling for those interested in different languages and dialects of Italy).

And then we took off on a hiking trail that connects Corniglia with Vernazza. The trail is in a good shape and is suitable for beginners, although the height difference might be tiresome for some. On the way, you get an understanding of the landscape and nature of the national park, local tradition of grape cultivation, great views of the sea and a lot of fun! At approximately midpoint between the two villages, we had a short stop in Prevo, where we enjoyed a refreshing mixed lemon and orange juice. The outside terrace has a picturesque view of Corniglia from a distance and it's worth a quick look. Continuing on our trail we approached Vernazza approximately 2h after we departed from Corniglia. The view over Vernazza with its eye-catching little castle is definitely worth a few photos.

We walked down into the village and, compared to the hiking trail where we barely met people, Vernazza seemed overly crowded! As everywhere in Cinque Terre once you come down to the water you see people enjoying their beach time without any beach though towels spread on the rocks, in the little harbour, on the pier, everywhere! Tired from the hiking and heated by the strong sun (around 30'C that day), we found refreshment in a pebble beach, where we had a short swim before taking the train to our next point of interest. To access the beach we had to go through a low natural tunnel (cave, actually) in the rock, with houses built on top of it. Of course, the tunnel was closed for access and of course that's where everyone was tempted to go! The beach was less crowded (maybe because of the don't-go-there sign?) and we could enjoy some time at the water. If you dare to go there, don't forget your swimming shoes!

Monterosso is probably the most popular of Cinque Terre. Maybe because it's the only one with a few sandy beaches, which make access to the sea more convenient (especially for kids and older people). As you come out of the train station, there is a nice street ("lungomare" in Italian) that goes along the beach. A bit of riviera-style, you can find small shops, "focaccerie" (where they sell a local type of pizza), "gelaterie" ("gelato" is the Italian for ice-cream), etc. Lungomare is nice for a stroll, it gives you that summer-resort feeling, but a bit overcrowded to my taste.

Honestly, I went to Cinque Terre to admire its nature, so Monterosso was not my favourite. But if you happen to be there and you are up for a bit of hiking, you should definitely head west towards Punta Mesco.

We started around 5 pm when everything around is just breathing heat after the sunny day. We found the hiking a bit heavy, perhaps because we were already quite tired of the day and because of the high temperature.

What unfolded in front of us when we reached the top made the extra effort definitely worth it! From the top you can enjoy a staggering view, not only of Monterosso but of all the five villages along the coast. If you are looking for a hike among the pines and for some break away from the crowds that's the thing to do! Advice: by the late afternoon you will get the perfect light for amazing pics, but don't be too late or the sun will hide behind the mountain.

Third Day: Manarola & Riomaggiore

The day after, we decided to take a break from hiking. We headed to Manarola by train. If you have ever googled Cinque Terre, the very first picture you see is taken in Manarola.

It's a lovely place that you find after walking through the tunnel that connects the station with the village. The narrow street going downhill leads to a small bay, where a mix of rocks and a small marina create a very picturesque view. But if you are after that very same Instagram killer-shot (that is probably the very reason you decided to book this trip), then you need to walk a few extra meters. Follow the crowd to the right of the bay, where a walking path leads you to the best view point. Afternoon/evening time is what you want for the classic sun-lit shot. But of course day light does not make the view less amazing. If you want to take a swim in Manarola, it is again a bit of rocky experience, right in the bay or behind the view point on the other side.

After Manarola, we headed to Riomaggiore, also by local train. Riomaggiore is another lovely village with direct access to the sea. Don't miss out on "fritto misto" in one of the shops in the central street. We got one from Il Pescato Cucinato, it was yummy! The layout of the village is on both sides of a little bay with a local marina. If you are a photographer, you might be even interested in renting a boat in the evening as the view from the sea after dark should be amazing. As all the other places, Riomaggiore is crowded in high season. I have heard of some tourists who woke up at 5am to see Cinque Terre without people but we didn't go that far.

In the past, it was possible to walk to Riomaggiore from Manarola following the famous Via dell'Amore but after its closure because of a landslide, only 200 meters were reopened above the train station. Don't be upset about it, other hiking trails offer beautiful summer views of the sea.

So here is how our short but active visit to Cinque Terre concluded. Riomaggiore and Manarola would both well deserve a longer visit, however, we also wanted to see the surrounding areas, so due to time constraints we had to head off to start our journey towards Portovenere and Portofino.

Cinque Terre offers almost any kind of vacation...from the relaxing and lovely views of its villages, up to kilometres of hiking trails for the more active tourists. It's a place that won't leave you indifferent to its beauty and if you combine it with the delicious Italian food experience, it will surely not disappoint you! What I realized is that after a couple of days visiting amazingly beautiful places, your eyes get almost used to such beauty, to the point that it feels as if you are not appreciating it anymore. Maybe that is just a little "bug" of my brain, or perhaps many, like me, would have such a thought. Anyways, always remind yourself of how lucky you are to be in such a place and that not everybody in the world will have your same opportunity to witness this

beauty during their lives

The End

Lightning Source UK Ltd.
Milton Keynes UK
UKHW020643240521
384271UK00011B/790